Donn Byrne
A Bibliography

Winthrop Wetherbee

Alpha Editions

This Edition Published in 2020

ISBN: 9789354216596

Design and Setting By
Alpha Editions
www.alphaedis.com
Email – info@alphaedis.com

As per information held with us this book is in Public Domain.
This book is a reproduction of an important historical work. Alpha Editions uses the best technology to reproduce historical work in the same manner it was first published to preserve its original nature. Any marks or number seen are left intentionally to preserve its true form.

Preface*

IN the preparation of a bibliography such as this, achievement of absolute completeness is an impossibility. Locating and recording every single item, by or about Donn Byrne, which has ever appeared in print anywhere, tracking down all the reviews, critical comment, and other notices concerning the books, short stories, poems and miscellaneous material, and especially, the identification of what must have been a large body of early writing by Byrne himself, is manifestly out of the question. Therefore, while it is hoped that errors of commission will be found to be infrequent in the following pages, those of omission must necessarily be many.

While the same comment could be said to apply with almost equal truth to any other bibliography, it is particularly applicable in the case of an author like Donn Byrne, who, to quote one critic, took no pains to annotate himself for posterity. Again, time and circumstances have combined to prohibit the following-up of many leads which might have been productive had they been approached earlier. The total destruction by bombing of the

---

* *Editor's note:* Except for the reference material cited, this bibliography is practically a catalogue of the compiler's collection of works by and about Donn Byrne. In gathering these, Dr. Wetherbee combed the usual sources and also visited every locality in America, Great Britain and Europe with which Byrne had been associated. Many items, including Byrne's own scrapbooks, were acquired in Ireland from Mrs. Byrne.

The patience, skill and devotion represented in the bibliography and the collection will be appreciated by everyone who, however modestly, has made a similar attempt. Dr. Wetherbee has paid rich tribute to Donn Byrne and lightened the task of all who may study his life and work. He has made this fine collection, complete in known published work and representative in manuscripts, readily available to students of literature by presenting it to The New York Public Library.

The bibliography as published here has been somewhat condensed from the original manuscript, both in the form of entries and by the omission of some references to such general works as the *Readers' Guide, International Index,* etc., and most of the minor newspaper and periodical reviews. Before editing, the whole of the original typescript was put on microfilm by the Library and positive prints of the film may be obtained through its Photographic Service.

PREFACE

records of Messrs. Sampson Low is one example of this; another, that with the passage of time, many of Donn Byrne's contemporaries, and many more of his older friends, are no longer available for interrogation concerning his early writing and other activities. Finally, the compiler must admit that the demands made on his own time by professional and extra-professional activities have frequently interrupted the progress of this book, and have therefore caused the end-result to be a spare-time, amateur production rather than the finished professional piece of work which such a subject deserves.

It is earnestly hoped that coming upon this bibliography may give an impetus to some future researcher to do further work on the subject. A biography, more complete than that of Mr. Macauley, could well be written; there is need, too, for a more exhaustive and detailed literary evaluation than has to date appeared in print. As for bibliography, there are so many unanswered questions that those mentioned in Note 2 of the Appendix merely give an indication of them. It is more in the hope of uncovering new material and new knowledge concerning Donn Byrne, than with the expectation of providing it, that this compilation has been made.

Although, strictly speaking, there is but a single "first edition" of any given book, for each of the Byrne titles there are cited in the following pages the first American edition, the first English edition, the limited edition, if any, and, in some cases, subsequent reprintings by other publishers.

Sufficient data are given, in each instance, to enable the reader to determine which is the true First Edition, in the bibliographic sense of the word.

The specific authority for the publication dates given for the several books is not cited in each case. These have been determined from the various trade publications such as *Publishers' Weekly* and *Publishers' Circular,* from correspondence with D.

PREFACE

Appleton-Century Company and Sampson Low, Marston & Company, and, in a few instances, from reviews which appeared, and so state, on the date of publication.

It is a pleasure to acknowledge indebtedness to the editors and publishers of the standard works of literary reference and bibliography in the United States and England. All such works have been searched and have been of considerable assistance in preparing this material.

Editors of the following periodicals have been kind enough to provide lists of Byrne material which appeared in their pages, and wherever in this volume reference is made to any of these journals, the credit is theirs:

America; The Buffalo (N. Y.) *News; The Canadian Bookman;* The Chicago *Tribune; The Christian Advocate; The Christian Register; The Churchman; The English Journal; The Grand Magazine; The Junior League Magazine;* the London *Daily Express;* the London *Daily Mail;* the London *Mercury;* the Montreal *Star; The New Republic; The New Statesman & Nation;* the Newport (R. I.) *News; The Spectator;* the Worcester (Mass.) *Telegram; The World Review.*

Members of the staffs of the D. Appleton-Century Co., Little, Brown & Co., The McCall Corporation, and the Frank A. Munsey Co. have furnished helpful contributions.

Finally, it is with particular pleasure that grateful indebtedness is acknowledged to the following individuals, all of whom have brought forward material of great value for the present compilation. Except for Mr. Price, who rightly heads the list, the names are listed alphabetically rather than according to number or importance of their additions: Messrs. J. McD. Price, Jr., Achmed Abdullah, Edward C. Aswell, Ernest A. Baker; Mrs. E. P. Berry; Messrs. Jacob Blanck, William A. Colescott, W. M. Clayton; Miss Georgina B. Davids; Messrs. Philip C. Duschnes, Paul Hervey Fox, Laurence J. Gomme, A. Herbert Greenberg;

PREFACE

Mrs. Sewell Haggard; Messrs. James A. Healey, Harold B. Hersey, Benjamin D. Hitz, Robert Lynd, Lee W. Maxwell, James A. McCann; Mrs. P. D. Perkins; Messrs. John A. Reed, Benjamin F. Shambaugh, Edward F. Smith, Albert Sperisen, James R. K. Taylor, Charles W. Thompson, Thomas J. Tiernan, J. C. Walsh, John Wilstach. Mrs. Dorothy Donn Byrne has been of inestimable help, and Dr. J. J. Nolan, Registrar of the National University, Dublin, has provided much information regarding Donn Byrne's student days, when they were undergraduates together.

WINTHROP WETHERBEE, Jr.

Table of Contents

Preface	v
The Books in Chronological Order:	
Stories Without Women	1
The Strangers' Banquet	5
The Foolish Matrons	6
Messer Marco Polo	8
The Wind Bloweth	11
Changeling, and Other Stories	13
Blind Raftery	17
O'Malley of Shanganagh — An Untitled Story	19
Hangman's House	21
Brother Saul	23
Crusade	25
Destiny Bay	27
Ireland, the Rock Whence I Was Hewn	29
Field of Honor — The Power of the Dog	31
A Party of Baccarat — The Golden Goat	33
Rivers of Damascus	35
A Woman of the Shee — Sargasso Sea	37
The Island of Youth	38
An Alley of Flashing Spears	40
The Hound of Ireland	42
A Daughter of the Medici	43
Poems	45

TABLE OF CONTENTS

The Short Stories:
    Short Stories Not Reprinted in Book Form   48
    Alphabetical List of Short Stories   50

Miscellaneous Writings   53

Translations   59

Anthologies   61

Dramatizations   63

Cinematizations   64

General Reference List   68

Appendix, *Notes*   85

DONN BYRNE
A BIBLIOGRAPHY

The Books in Chronological Order

STORIES WITHOUT WOMEN

Hearst's International Library Co., 1915 (November)

Stories | Without | Women | (And A Few With Women) | By | Donn Byrne | "To encourage all valorous hearts and to shew | them honorable examples." | — Froissart | [publisher's device] | Illustrated | Hearst's International Library Co. | New York 1915

Collation: 12mo (19½ × 13½ cm.). 330 p. End paper; flyleaf, half-title [1], Stories without women; verso blank; frontispiece inset opposite title page; title page [3], as above, in three compartments, formed by double rules; verso [4], Copyright, 1915, by | Hearst's International Library Co. | All rights reserved, including that of translation into the foreign languages, including the Scandinavian; [5] To | My wife, Dorothy, | These old friends; [6] publisher's acknowledgments; [7] contents | Chapter Page | list of titles; [8] blank; 9–330, text, followed by six blank unnumbered pages, blank flyleaf, and end paper. Frontispiece by T. D. Skidmore. $1.25.

Binding: Bound in red cloth with white lettering as follows: *Backstrip:* Stories | Without | Women | [rule] | Byrne | H. I. L. Co. *Front cover:* Stories | Without | Women | Donn Byrne   Back cover blank; white end papers; all edges cut.

The Century Co., 1931 (January 30)

Stories | Without Women | And a Few With Women | By | Donn Byrne | * | "To encourage all valorous | hearts and to show them | honorable examples." | Froissart | [publisher's device] | The Century Co. | New York   London

Collation: 12mo (19½ × 13½ cm.). ix, 309 p. End paper and flyleaf; [i] half-title: Stories Without Women | (And A Few With Women); verso [ii], blank; [iii] title page, as above; [iv] Copyright, 1915, by | Hearst International Library Co. | Copyright, 1931, by the Century Co. | All rights reserved, including the | right to reproduce this book, or | portions thereof, in any form | First printing | Printed in U. S. A.; [v] To | My Wife, Dorothy | These old friends; [vi] blank; [vii] publisher's acknowledgments; [viii] blank; [ix] Contents | Chapter Page (list of titles follows); [x] blank; [1] Stories Without Women | (And A Few With Women); [2] blank; 3–309, text; [310], (verso) blank, flyleaf and end paper. Not illustrated. $2.00.

Binding: Bound in rust brown cloth with black lettering as follows: *Backstrip:* Stories | Without | Women | [ornament] | Donn | Byrne | The | Century | Co. Double rules at top and bottom. *Front cover:* Stories | Without | Women | [ornament] | Donn | Byrne   Double rules with ornaments in corners. Back cover blank; light brown endpapers and flyleaf; yellow top; all edges cut.

DONN BYRNE BIBLIOGRAPHY

Sampson Low, Marston & Co., Ltd., 1931 (January 19)

Stories | Without Women | (And a Few With Women) | By | Donn Byrne | London | Sampson Low, Marston & Co., Ltd.

Collation: 12mo (19 x 13 cm.). v, 282 p. End paper; flyleaf; [i] half-title: Stories Without Women | (And a Few With Women); [ii] list of other works by Mr. Donn Byrne | First Impression; [iii] title page, as above; [iv] Made and printed in Great Britain by Purnell and Sons | Paulton (Somerset) and London; v, Contents | page (list of titles follows); [vi] blank; 1–282, text, followed by flyleaf and end paper. Not illustrated. 7/6.

Binding: Bound in black cloth, with lettering as follows: *Backstrip* (gilt): Stories | Without | Women | Donn | Byrne | Sampson Low   A narrow gilt line runs across backstrip ½ cm. from top and lower edges.   *Front cover* (blind stamped): Stories | Without Women | Donn Byrne   Back cover blank; white end papers; all edges cut.

The publisher issued a cheaper edition, 1932 (March), 3/6.

Contents: Biplane no. 2. Slaves of the gun. In a cellar. Bow Sing Low and the two who were thieves. An African epic. A man's game. Donoghu's hour. Jungle bulls. The wake. Out of Egypt. Black medicine. Panic. The story of Suleyman Bey.

First editions:
Hearst's. Date on title page (single printing).
Century. "First printing" on copyright page.
Sampson Low. "First impression" opposite title page.

Periodical publication:
Biplane no. 2. *Century magazine*, 88:5, p. 716–720; September, 1914. Not illustrated

Slaves of the gun. *Smart set*, 43:3, p. 75–81; July, 1914. Not illustrated.
In a cellar. *Smart set*, 43:1, p. 113–119; May, 1914. Not illustrated.
Bow Sing Low and the two who were thieves. *All-story magazine*, 48:4, p. 731–739; August 28, 1915. Not illustrated. Magazine title: Two who were thieves.
Donoghu's hour. *Smart set*, 43:4, p. 123–130; August, 1914. Not illustrated. (Also, in abbreviated version, in *Current opinion*, 58:3, p. 203–205; March, 1915. Not illustrated.)
An African epic. *Smart set*, 43:2, p. 119–124; June, 1914. Not illustrated.
A man's game. *Popular magazine*, 35.6, p. 197–206; March 7, 1915. Not illustrated. Magazine title: Inside stuff.
Jungle bulls. *American Sunday monthly magazine*, September 5, 1915, p. 9–13. Illustrated by T. D. Skidmore.
The wake. *Harper's magazine*, 131:785, p. 758–762; October, 1915. Not illustrated.
Out of Egypt. Apparently, no prior magazine publication (see notes at end of this section).
Black medicine. *Popular magazine*, 35:4, p. 199–209; February 7, 1915. Not illustrated.
Panic. *All-story magazine*, 45:3, p. 539–547; May 29, 1915. Not illustrated.
The story of Suleyman Bey. *Romance*, 6:1, p. 85–93; July, 1915. Not illustrated.

STORIES WITHOUT WOMEN

The 1915 edition is the rarest of the Donn Byrne books. Only 639 copies are reported to have been sold, and of these, the author himself bought thirteen. No copy in mint condition, with the original dust jacket, is known to exist; only two in the original wrappers have been offered at public auction. Of the two copies in the Treasure Room of the Harvard College Library, neither has the dust jacket, and both are in poor condition. The present writer has made an attempt to locate as many as possible of the thirteen copies which Mr. Byrne purchased, presumably for presentation to friends, and assumes that the following are among them:

1. An uninscribed copy, presented to Mr. James R. K. Taylor, and still in his possession (personal communication from Mr. Taylor).

2. Copy inscribed by the author for Carl Gauss (see Scribner catalogue no. 122, item 34).

3. Presentation copy to Joyce Kilmer (see Argus Book Shop "Along the North Wall," section six, 1937, p. 47).

4. Presentation copy inscribed to Mr. E. J. Fay (in possession of the Wetherbee Collection). Mr. Fay was the Byrnes' landlord while they were living in Columbia Heights, Brooklyn, in 1915–1916.

5. Copy inscribed to Mr. J. A. McCann (see Parke-Bernet Galleries catalogue no. 140, of sale November 15–16, 1939).

In connection with the above copy, the catalogue wherein it is described states: "This is believed to be the only known presentation copy of this work in existence." It further quotes a letter from Mr. McCann, in part as follows: "... The edition was very small — less than 400 copies were sold, and the unsold remainder was destroyed shortly after it was published. The book is now almost extinct. Shortly before Byrne died I spoke to him about this autographed copy, and he advised me that he knew of no existing autographed *Stories without women*. Since then I have spoken to both his friends and literary advisers and have been told that the book is hard to get and that an autographed copy has never been seen."

6. Uninscribed copy, with many contemporary review clippings tipped in, believed to have been Donn Byrne's own copy (also mentioned in letter referred to above). In possession of the Wetherbee Collection.

7. Copy inscribed to Bernard Metts (see American Art Association-Anderson Galleries catalogue no. 4201, November 13–14, 1935, item 45). This catalogue gives the name of the recipient, incorrectly, as "Betts"; Mr. Metts was a Dutchman with whom Donn Byrne became acquainted during a visit to Bermuda in 1916.

Notes on individual stories:

Biplane No. 2. This story leads all of the others in the amount of critical comment it received. Mr. Macauley refers to it as "a fine war story," and many commentators have remarked that it is surprisingly little "dated." Jessup's *Representative American short stories* mentions it, as does Baker's *Contemporary short story*. O'Brien's *Best short stories* (1915) gives it two asterisks, indicating more than ordinary distinction, and Blanche Colton Williams, in her *Handbook on story writing* also makes specific reference to it.

In a cellar. Specifically referred to in twelve reviews. Of interest as the first of many of the author's stories dealing with Jewish subjects.

DONN BYRNE BIBLIOGRAPHY

Bow Sing Low and the two who were thieves. In the Metts presentation copy of *Stories without women,* referred to above, Mr Metts has pencilled some brief notes giving the author's comments on the various stories. Opposite "Bow Sing Low" is the note "D. B. says the best."

A man's game. Also discussed by Harry T. Baker in *The contemporary short story.*

Jungle bulls. Mr. Metts' pencilled notation: "D. B. says bad."

The wake. Reprinted in O'Brien's *Best short stories of 1915.*

In a letter written from Martha's Vineyard, June 30, 1918, Donn Byrne expresses the following opinion: "...A story is a story whether it's a novel of 100,000 words or a short magazine affair. There is no difference in technic between a 4,000 word writing like The Wake and any of my big 15,000 worders in the *Saturday Evening Post* ... The short story is to the novel what the chip mashie shot is to the full St. Andrews swing, the same identical stroke used effectively for shorter distance ... "

The author received $75 00 from *Harper's* for this story.

"The Wake" is mentioned specifically in half a dozen of the reviews, is discussed in several of Mr. Macauley's writings, and is referred to at some length by Mr. O'Brien in his 1915 volume Miss Williams devotes considerable space to it in her *How to study "The best short stories."*

Out of Egypt. In the *Stories without women* publisher's acknowledgment, one of the periodicals mentioned is *Every week.* As all of the short stories in the volume, except "Out of Egypt," have been located in other magazines, it appears that this story must have been sold to *Every week.* However, a careful check of the files fails to reveal this or any other story by Donn Byrne, and the assumption must be made that the magazine bought the story but never published it.

The magazine had a short life. Vol. 1, no. 1 appeared May 3, 1915, and vol. 6, no. 25 (the last published), June 22, 1918. It was brought out by the Crowell Publishing Co., under the editorship of Bruce Barton, and sold for 3 cents per copy. Among the friends of Donn Byrne who contributed to it were George Bronson-Howard, Arthur Somers Roche, and Paul Hervey Fox.

Black medicine. Donn Byrne's comment, as recorded by Mr. Metts: "Very bad. D. B."

In the *Popular magazine* of June 20, 1916, on p. 54, Donn Byrne is referred to as the author of a story entitled "Black magic." A careful search through the periodical literature has failed to reveal any story of this title, and it is presumed therefore that the reference is properly to "Black medicine." This presumption is more or less substantiated by the fact that it was in the *Popular magazine* that the latter story was published, and also by the occurrence in the same magazine, June 7, 1915, of a similar "blurb" which refers to the story by its correct title. Of coincidental interest is the title of the motion picture "Black magic" in the short story "Anti-climax."

The American Art Association-Anderson Galleries catalogue which describes the Metts presentation copy mentions notes which indicate that some of the stories were translated into other languages. The present compiler has been unable to consult the volume in question, and therefore cannot state which stories were thus treated, into what languages they were translated, or where the translations appeared.

THE STRANGERS' BANQUET

Reviews: The Times literary supplement, London, v. 30, April 2, 1931, p. 268; *New York Times book review,* v. 4, no. 18, May 17, 1931, p. 3; *Saturday review of literature,* v. 7, no. 33, March 7, 1931, p. 651; *New York Evening Post,* Jan. 31, 1931 (Edwin Seaver).

THE STRANGERS' BANQUET
Harper & Brothers, 1919 (December)

The Strangers' | Banquet | By Donn Byrne | "There is an evil which I have seen under the sun, | and it is common among men: A man to whom | God hath given riches, wealth, and honor, so that | he wanteth nothing for his soul of all that he | desireth ... but a stranger eateth it: this is vanity | and it is an evil disease." — The words of the | Preacher, the son of David, king in Jerusalem. [quotation is in italics] | [publisher's device] | Harper & Brothers Publishers | New York and London

Collation: 12mo (19 x 13 cm.). 352 p. End paper; flyleaf; blank page with blank verso; half-title: The Strangers' | Banquet; verso blank; title page, as above; verso: The Strangers' Banquet | [rule] | Copyright, 1919, by Harper & Brothers | Printed in the United States of America | Published December, 1919 | M-T; [vii] To | Sewell Haggard; verso, blank; [1] The Strangers' | Banquet; verso, quotation as on title page; 3–352, text; followed by blank flyleaf and end paper. Not illustrated. $1.75.

Binding: Bound in rough black cloth, lettered in gilt, as follows: *Backstrip:* The | Strangers' | Banquet | Donn | Byrne | Harpers   *Front cover:* The Strangers' | Banquet | Donn Byrne | Back cover blank; white end papers; all edges cut.

First edition: At foot of copyright page, "Published December, 1919," and code letters "M-T." Black cloth, with lettering in gilt. Single printing.

Reprint

New York: Grosset & Dunlap, 1921. 19 x 13cm. 352 p. 75 cents.

Reprinted, 1923, illustrated with scenes from the photoplay.

A personal communication from Messrs. Harper and Brothers states that the first printing of this book consisted of 7,500 copies, was printed October 31, 1919, and that no subsequent edition was published by this firm.

The manuscript of *The Strangers' banquet* was sold at auction in New York on February 25, 1938, and is described in the Parke-Bernet Galleries catalogue no. 11 of that date.

This novel was made into a motion picture, details concerning which will be found in the "Cinematizations" section.

The following presentation copies are known to exist:
1. The copy inscribed to Carl F. Gauss, described in the catalogue of the Parke-Bernet Galleries, no. 13, March 3, 1938 (item 18, p. 4).
2. Copy inscribed to Tom Walsh, described in American Art Association-Anderson Galleries catalogue no. 4253, April 22-23, 1936 (item 61, p. 21).

In "The Gossip shop" column of *The Bookman* for March, 1920 (51:1, p. 126) there is brief mention of Donn Byrne and of *The Strangers' banquet;* in the issue of April, 1920 (51:2, p. 253) there is noted the author's refusal to sell the rights to this story for purposes of serialization.

Reviews: The Dial, v. 68, no. 4, April, 1920, p. 536; *New York Tribune,* Dec. 20, 1919, p. 9; *New York Evening Post,* Jan. 3, 1920, book section, p. 4.

THE FOOLISH MATRONS

Harper & Brothers, 1920 (September)

The Foolish | Matrons | By Donn Byrne | "Every wise woman buildeth her | house: but the foolish plucketh it | down with her hands." | — The Book called Proverbs [quotation is in italics] | [publisher's device] | Harper & Brothers Publishers | New York and London

Collation: 12mo (19 x 13 cm.). 384 p. End paper; flyleaf with blank verso; [i] half-title: The Foolish Matrons; verso [ii], blank; [iii] title page, as above; verso [iv], The Foolish Matrons | Copyright, 1920, by Harper & Brothers | Printed in the United States of America | Published September, 1920 | I-N; [v] The Players ask for a Blessing | on the Psalteries and Themselves (above in italics) | "... O kinsmen of the Three in One | O Kinsmen bless the hands that play. | The notes they waken shall live on | When all this heavy history's done; | Our hands, our hands must ebb away. | ... The proud and careless notes live on, | But bless our hands that ebb away." | W. B. Yeats; verso [vi], blank: [vii] Contents; verso [viii], blank; [1] Book I | The Book Of The Building House; verso [2], blank; 3-384, text; followed by blank flyleaf and end paper. Not illustrated. $2.00.

Binding: Bound in green cloth, lettered in black, as follows: *Backstrip:* The | Foolish | Matrons | By | Donn | Byrne | Harpers   *Front:* The | Foolish | Matrons | By | Donn Byrne (the whole enclosed in black stamped shield). Back cover blank; white end papers; all edges cut.

Sampson Low, Marston & Co., Ltd., 1923 (September 18)

The Foolish | Matrons | By | Donn Byrne | Author of | "The Wind Bloweth," "Messer Marco Polo" | "Every wise woman buildeth her | house: but the foolish plucketh it | down with her hands." | — The Book Called Proverbs | [publisher's device] | London | Sampson Low, Marston & Co., Ltd.

Collation: 12mo (19 x 13 cm.). 313 p. End paper and flyleaf; [i] half-title: The Foolish Matrons; verso [ii], blank; [iii] title page, as above; verso [iv], Printed

THE FOOLISH MATRONS

in Great Britain by Purnell and Sons ¦ Paulton, Somerset, England; [v] Contents; verso [vi], blank; 1–313, text; followed by one blank unnumbered page, flyleaf, and end paper. Not illustrated. 7/6.

Binding: Bound in bright red cloth, lettered in black as follows: *Backstrip:* The | Foolish | Matrons | Donn | Byrne | Sampson Low   *Front:* The | Foolish Matrons | Donn Byrne   A narrow black line runs across backstrip ½ cm. from top and lower edges; front cover bears a similar line forming a rectangle ½ cm. from edges. Back cover is blank; white end papers; all edges cut.

Reprinted, uniform edition, 1931 (February). 3/6; cheaper editions, 1931 (July); 1935 (August, September). 2/6.

First editions:

Harper. At bottom of copyright page, "Published September, 1920," and code letters "I–U." Bound in light or dark green cloth, with no known priority. A personal communication from Messrs. Harper & Brothers states that the first edition, consisting of 5,000 copies, was printed August 31, 1920, and that there was a second printing of 750 copies on April 19, 1921, but that they have no information regarding the different colors of the binding.

Sampson Low. The first printing bears no date, and there is no statement as to the printing; the volume is bound in bright red cloth, with black lettering. Subsequent printings are so marked, and in addition, are bound in black cloth.

The manuscript of *The Foolish matrons* was sold at auction in New York on February 25, 1938, and is described in the Parke-Bernet Galleries catalogue no. 11, of that date. A facsimile reproduction of the title page of this manuscript forms the frontispiece of the catalogue.

This novel is stated to have been translated into Italian, and published in that language in 1930. All available information concerning this is given in the section on "Translations."

Details concerning the motion picture will be found in the "Cinematizations" section.

The following presentation copies are known to be in existence:

1. Copy inscribed for Arnold Daly, as described in Argosy Book Stores catalogue no. 117, in the Wetherbee Collection. (The word "Nov." in the inscription, as given in the catalogue, should read "Noel.")

2. Copy of English first printing, inscribed: "For Admiral & Mrs. Hyde, Sincerely, Donn Byrne. Day of publication, September 18, 1923." (In the Wetherbee Collection.)

3. Another copy, as above, inscribed "For Mr. & Mrs. Wilson, with the author's compliments, Donn Byrne, July 3, 1924." The Wilsons were friends of the Byrnes at Walmer. (Also in the Wetherbee Collection.)

Reviews: New York Times, III, 24:4, Oct. 10, 1920; *The Bookman,* London, 65:385, p. 46, October, 1923; *New York Tribune,* VII, 8:1–2 (Samuel Abbott); *New York Evening Post literary review,* 1:6, p. 10, Oct. 16, 1920; *Times literary supplement,* London, v. 22, no. 605, Sept. 13, 1923.

DONN BYRNE BIBLIOGRAPHY

MESSER MARCO POLO

The Century Co., 1921 (October)

Messer | Marco Polo | By | Donn Byrne | Illustrated | By C. B. Falls | [publisher's device] | New York | The Century Co. | 1921

Collation. Narrow 12mo (19 x 11 cm.). 147 p. End paper; flyleaf and verso, blank, [i] blank; verso [ii], blank; [iii] half-title: Messer | Marco Polo; verso [iv], blank; frontispiece inset, facing title page; [v] title page, as above; verso [vi], Copyright, 1921, by | The Century Co. | Printed in U. S. A; [vii] list of illustrations; verso [viii], blank; [1] divisional half-title: Messer | Marco Polo; verso [2], blank; 3–147, text; followed by single blank page, flyleaf, and end paper. $1.25.

Binding: Bound in terra cotta cloth with black lettering, as follows: *Backstrip:* Mes- | ser | Mar- | co | Polo | Donn | Byrne | The | Century | Co. *Front:* Messer | Marco | Polo | By | Donn | Byrne. Solid black vertical line from top to lower edge of front and back covers, approximately 2½ cm. from back edge. White end papers; all edges cut.

The Century Co. published later printings of this book bound in black leather, with lettering in gilt, and gilt tops. These were uniform with the leather-bound editions of *Blind Raftery, O'Malley of Shanganagh,* and *A Party of baccarat.* None of the first printing were so bound.

The exact date of publication of the Century Co. edition of *Messer Marco Polo* has never been established, but in the opinion of the present writer it must have been very early in October, 1921, probably October 1 or October 2. While many reviews appeared in the periodical press during the preceding month, it is necessary to remember that the serialization in the *Century magazine* concluded with the October issue, which appeared actually in September, the earlier reviews frequently read as if they were derived from the magazine appearance rather than the subsequent publication in book form. The following references to the *Publishers' weekly* tend to support this contention:

September 17, 1921. Book is mentioned in a Century Co. advertisement on inside front cover, and on p. 818 there is brief mention of the book and its author, but with nothing to indicate that it had yet appeared in print other than in the *Century magazine.*

September 24, 1921. Listing in Index, and, on p. 911, a Century Co. advertisement which implies the release of advance copies to "critics and colyumnists," but not appearance on the bookstands.

October 8, 1921. Announcement in Weekly record, p. 1263. This probably the best indication of the true publication date, and would place it some time during the preceding week.

November 5, 1921. Century Co. advertisement (p. 24), and review (p. 75).

A personal communication from The Century Co., written in 1928, gives the following "publication dates," the first of which does not invalidate the above hypothesis, as these dates are almost certainly those of the printing orders rather than of actual placing on sale: July 28, 1921, November 14, 1921, December 16, 1921, February 18, 1922, July 14, 1922, December 4, 1922, February 2, 1923, July, 1923, November 16, 1923, March 31, 1924.

The first two of the above printings bear the date "1921" at bottom of title page; the third, although printed in 1921, bears the date "1922."

Sampson Low, Marston & Co., Ltd., 1922 (May 26)

Messer | Marco Polo | By | Donn Byrne | Illustrated | London | Sampson Low, Marston | And Co. Ltd.

Collation. Narrow 12mo (19 × 13 cm.). 151 p. End paper; flyleaf and verso, blank; [i] half-title· Messer | Marco Polo, verso [ii], blank; frontispiece in color, inset, facing title page; title page [iii], as above; verso, Copyright, 1921, by | The Century Co.; [v] List of illustrations; verso [vi], blank, [1] Divisional half-title. Messer | Marco Polo; verso [2], blank; 3–151, text; at bottom of p. 151: Jarrold & Sons, Limited, Printers, The Empire Press, Norwich.; followed by three pages of advertisements, blank flyleaf, and end paper. Frontispiece in color, and four black-and-white illustrations by C. B. Falls. 6/.

Binding: Bound in bright red cloth, lettered in black, as follows: *Backstrip:* Messer | Marco | Polo | Donn | Byrne | Sampson Low. *Front:* Messer Marco Polo | Donn Byrne. Narrow black line across backstrip, ½ cm. from top and lower edges; similar black line forming rectangle on front cover, inset ½ cm. from edges. Back cover blank. White end papers; all edges cut.

Reprinted, uniform edition, 1931 (February), 6/; cheaper edition, 1931 (July), 3/6; school reader edition, 1930 (June). This latter contains an abbreviated and otherwise altered version of the title story, and also the short stories "The Barnacle goose" and "The keeper of the bridge." Not illustrated. 122 p. 2/.

Reprints

New York: Random House, 1942 (November 2). No. 43 in the "Modern library" series of reprints. 95 cents.

New York: Editions for the Armed Services, Inc., 1943. No. F 151 in this series, published during World War II by the above organization, established by the Council on Books in War Time.

New York: Penguin Books, 1946 (October); no. 611. 25 cents.

A fine edition, with illustrations by Keye Luke, was to be published by D. Appleton-Century Co. in 1942, and publication for August 28th of that year was actually announced, but was subsequently cancelled due to wartime conditions.

First editions:

Century. Cloth; "1921" at bottom of title page; illustrations on heavier paper than in later editions; intact word "of," end of last line, p. 10; single blank page at end. The much published statement that the misspelled "forgetting" (forgettng) in line 3, p. 39, is a "point" is a mistake, as this error persists in all later printings up to and including the Random House reprint.

Sampson Low. Cloth (red, with black lettering); no date on title page; on copyright page "Copyright, 1921, The Century Co."; imperfect "that is," line 11, p. 126. Subsequent editions not illustrated.

DONN BYRNE BIBLIOGRAPHY

Periodical publication: Century magazine, v. 102, August – October, 1921, p. 480–494, 668–682, 820–834. Illustrated by C. B. Falls. The magazine publication of this story was illustrated with many more drawings than appeared in the later book.

Reprinted later in the *Golden book magazine*, v. 15, January – March, 1932, p. 18–30, 178–189, 272–283, with illustrations by John Alan Maxwell.

Condensed "capsule" versions appear in Helen R. Keller's *Readers' digest of books* (New York: Macmillan, 1936), and in the *World review* (Mt. Morris, Ill.) of September 27, 1926.

The illustration opposite p. 86 (Century ed.) was used in slightly reduced size ($2^7_8 \times 3\frac{1}{8}$ inches) by Donn Byrne as his personal bookplate. A double scroll was added at the base, inscribed "Ex libris Donn Byrne," and the whole printed in sepia. Mrs. Clare Ryan Talbot, the bookplate authority, reproduces this plate in her book on the subject

Interesting information concerning Donn Byrne's interest in Marco Polo, his sources for writing the book, and how he came to write it, will be found in the *Bookman*, New York, v. 54, January, 1922, The Contributors' column, p. [4] (letter from Mr. Maxwell Aley), and in the *Century magazine*, 105:4, adv.; February, 1923 ("The Centurion").

The manuscript of *Messer Marco Polo* was sold at auction in New York on April 18, 1934 The American Art Association-Anderson Galleries catalogue of this date contains a description of the manuscript, and, as frontispiece, a facsimile reproduction of the first page of the manuscript. It was subsequently presented to the Harvard College Library.

The following presentation copies are known:

1. First English edition, inscribed "To A. B. Bartly, Esq. Best of luck! Very sincerely yours, Donn Byrne. June, 1922." In the Wetherbee Collection.

2. Century Co. second printing, inscribed "To Amy Lowell, reverently, Donn Byrne. November, 1921." In Poetry Room of Harvard College Library.

3. First American edition, inscribed "To Sewell Haggard, Never forgetting that his advice, support, and encouragement made my best writing possible. Very sincerely, Donn Byrne. October 10, 1921." In possession of Mrs. Haggard.

4. Century Co. second printing, with Donn Byrne's card laid in, and inscribed: "Alfred W. Lublin, Esq. Greeting, for his seventy-third birthday. Donn Byrne." This copy must have been presented a number of years after the book was published, as the card bears the address "Coolmain Castle, Co. Cork." In the Wetherbee Collection.

5. Century Co. first printing inscribed: "To Herbert Hand, very cordially, Donn Byrne, Day of publication, 1921." In possession of Mr. Hand.

6. Century first edition, inscribed: "To Lovell M. Palmer, Jr. supporting Dan Parker's contention that he is a gentleman, a sportsman and a scholar! Sincerely, Donn Byrne. November, 1921." In Berg Collection, New York Public Library.

7. Century first printing, inscribed: "To S. Jay Kaufman, in memory of another Irish tale, 'General John Regan' — old ghostlike days! Cordially, Donn Byrne, October 31, 1921." In the Wetherbee Collection.

8. The James L. Ford presentation copy described in Parke-Bernet Galleries catalogue of sale January 23–24, 1945 (item 53, p. 14). This is stated to be first printing of the Century Co. edition.

THE WIND BLOWETH

Reviews: The Bookman, New York, v. 54, December, 1921, p. 396 (Heywood Broun); *The Dial,* v. 71, December, 1921, p. 714; *New York Times book review,* Oct. 9, 1921, III, 18:2; *New York Evening Post literary review,* Oct. 15, 1921, p. 84; *Judge,* v. 81, Dec. 17, 1921, p. 28 (Walter Prichard Eaton); *Atlantic monthly,* v. 129, Feb., 1922, p. 2, 10, 12 (Katherine Lee Bates); *The Nation,* New York, v. 113, Nov. 2, 1921, p. 506 (James Branch Cabell). Mr. Cabell re-evaluates his *Nation* review in the following publications: (a) in his *Straws and prayerbooks,* New York, 1924, p. 52–59, and (b) in *Reading and collecting,* Chicago, v. 1, no. 11, Oct., 1937, p. 7–8.

THE WIND BLOWETH
The Century Co., 1922 (September)

The | Wind Bloweth | By | Donn Byrne | Author of "Messer Marco Polo," etc. | Illustrated By | George Bellows | [publisher's device] | New York | The Century Co. | 1922

Collation: 12mo (19 x 13 cm.). 393 p. End paper; flyleaf and verso blank; frontispiece inset facing title page [i], as above; verso [ii], Copyright, 1922, by | The Century Co. | Printed in U. S. A.; [iii–iv] A Dedication: A Prayer; [v] Contents; verso [vi], blank; [1] divisional half-title: Part One | Dancing Town; verso [2], blank; 3–393, text; followed by single blank page, flyleaf, and end paper. $2.00.

Binding: Bound in terra cotta cloth, lettered in black, as follows: *Backstrip:* The | Wind | Bloweth | Donn | Byrne | The | Century | Co. *Front cover:* The Wind | Bloweth | Donn | Byrne Backstrip has double black line 2½ cm. from top and lower edges; a similar double line encloses the lettering on the front cover, extending horizontally 2½ cm. from edges, and vertically 2 cm. from edges. Back cover blank; white end papers; all edges cut.

A personal communication from the Century Co., in November, 1928, gives the following dates of printings of *The Wind bloweth:* July 31, 1922, December 4, 1922, March 5, 1923, November 13, 1923. These are the dates of the various printing orders, rather than those of actual publication; first edition appeared on the stands during the last week of September, 1922.

Sampson Low, Marston & Co., Inc., 1922 (November)

The | Wind Bloweth | [rule] | By | Donn Byrne | Author of Messer Marco Polo | [quotation from The Gospel According to St. John] | [publisher's device] | [rule] | London: | Sampson Low, Marston & Co., Ltd.

Collation: 12mo (19 x 13 cm.). End paper; flyleaf and verso, blank; [i] half-title, The Wind Bloweth; verso [ii], blank; [iii] title page, as above, the whole enclosed in a rectangle formed of single black lines; verso [iv], Printed in Great Britain by Fox, Jones & Co., | Kemp Hall Press, High Street, Oxford, England.; [v] To | Madame Dorothea Donn-Byrne; verso [vi], blank; [vii]

Contents; verso [viii], blank, [1] divisional half-title: Book One | Dancing Town | B; verso [2], blank; 3–310, text, followed by eight (unnumbered) pages of advertisements; blank flyleaf and verso, end paper. Not illustrated. 7/6.

Binding. Bound in bright red cloth, lettered in black, as follows: *Backstrip:* The Wind Bloweth | Donn | Byrne | Sampson Low Narrow black lines across backstrip, 1½ cm. from top and lower edges. *Front cover:* The Wind Bloweth Donn Byrne   Narrow black line ½ cm. from edges, forming a rectangle on cover, enclosing lettering. White end papers; all edges cut.

Reprinted, uniform edition, 1931 (February), 7/6; cheaper editions, 1931 (March, July), 3/6.

Reprint

New York: Grosset & Dunlap Co., 1929. "Novels of distinction" series. 20 × 14 cm. 393 p. Illustrated by George Bellows. $1.00.

First editions:
Century. Misprint, line 20, p. 151, "money," later corrected to "honey."
Sampson Low. No date or statement as to printing. Bound in bright red cloth; subsequent printings bound in black.

Periodical publication. The Century magazine, v. 103, April, 1922, p. 803–824; v. 104, May – October, 1922, p. 96–116, 229–252, 435–458, 602–623, 757–780, 917–932.

The magazine publication contains many more illustrations (seventeen) by George Bellows than are included in the later volume. The latter is said to be one of only two volumes for which Mr. Bellows did the illustrations. Donn Byrne and George Bellows were quite friendly at one period, the latter admired *The Wind Bloweth* immensely, and mutual interest in other subjects, notably prize-fighting, gave them much in common. Mr. Bellows did a fine drawing of Donn Byrne, which was reproduced in the *Century magazine* of April, 1922. Neither Mrs. Byrne nor Mrs. Bellows has any recollection of the fate of the original, nor has the Century Company been able to furnish this information.

The "A Dedication: A Prayer" which appears at the front of the Century volume is omitted from the Sampson Low edition, the latter being dedicated simply "To Madame Dorothea Donn-Byrne." In the *Century magazine,* this Dedication does not appear as part of the text, but is printed in the front advertising pages of the April issue, together with the gospel quotation from which the title is derived. This quotation does not appear in the Century Co. volume.

The last page of the Sampson Low volume bears the inscription "America, 1920–1922," which is not present in the *Century magazine* or the Century Co. book. Actually, the manuscript was completed December 29, 1921, and is so dated in Donn Byrne's hand.

The title which Donn Byrne originally had in mind for the book was one which he had previously used for a short story which appeared in the *Saturday evening post* in 1918 — "Fiddler's Green." In the *Bookman* for October, 1921 (54, p. 185–186) is a publisher's "blurb" which describes him as being busily engaged in writing "Fiddler's Green" at Riverside; there is a similar article in the *Century* for December, 1921 (103:2, adv.).

CHANGELING, AND OTHER STORIES

The manuscript was sold at auction in New York April 14, 1937, and is described in the American Art Association-Anderson Galleries catalogue of that date.

To the best of this compiler's knowledge and belief, no inscribed presentation copy has ever been offered at public auction; neither has he any knowledge of any such copies privately owned.

The episode entitled "The Wrestler from Aleppo" is included in Fulcher's *Short narratives* (see under "Anthologies").

The book has been done into Braille; details regarding this may be found in the section "Translations."

Reviews: New York Evening Post literary review, October 28, 1922, p. 144 (Stephen Vincent Benét), *New York Times*, Oct. 1, 1922, III, 22:1; *The Nation*, New York, v. 115, Nov. 8, 1922, p. 503 (Joseph Wood Krutch); *New York Tribune*, Oct. 8, 1922, v, 8:8; *The Bookman*, London, v. 63, December, 1922, p. 168–169; *The Spectator*, London, v. 130, Jan. 13, 1923, p. 67; *The Bookman*, New York, v. 56, December, 1922, p. 493 (John V. A. Weaver); *The Times literary supplement*, London, v. 21, Nov. 9, 1922, p. 279.

CHANGELING, AND OTHER STORIES

The Century Co., 1923 (September 28)

Changeling | And Other Stories | By | Donn Byrne | Author of "The Wind Bloweth," "Messer | Marco Polo," etc. | [publisher's device] | New York & London | The Century Co.

Collation: 12mo (19 x 13 cm.). 418 p. End paper; flyleaf and verso, blank; [i] and verso [ii], blank, [iii] half-title: Changeling | And Other Stories; verso [iv], blank; [v] title page, as above. Lettering is enclosed in rectangle formed by double lines, of which the inner is narrower; [vi] Copyright, 1923, by | The Century Co. | Printed in U. S. A.; [vii] Dedication, continued on [viii]; [ix] Contents; verso [x], blank; [1], divisional half-title: Changeling and Other Stories; verso [2], blank; 3–418, text; followed by four blank unnumbered pages, flyleaf and end paper. Not illustrated. $2.50.

Binding: Bound in terra cotta cloth, with black lettering as follows: *Backstrip:* Change- | ling | [ornament] | Donn | Byrne | The | Century | Co. Triple black lines across backstrip, ½ cm. from top and lower edges. *Front cover:* Changeling | And Other Stories | Donn Byrne   Blind stamped border forming a rectangle inset 1 cm. from edges of cover. Back cover blank; white end papers; all edges cut.

Sampson Low, Marston & Co., Ltd., 1924 (October)

Changeling | And Other Stories | By | Donn Byrne | Author of | "The Wind Bloweth," "Messer Marco Polo," | "Foolish Matrons," etc. | [publisher's device] | London | Sampson Low, Marston & Co., Ltd.

Collation: 12mo (19 x 13 cm.). End paper; flyleaf and verso, blank; [i] half-title: Changeling | And Other Stories; verso [ii], blank; [iii], title page, as above;

[iv] Printed in Great Britain by Purnell and Sons | Paulton, Somerset, England; v–vi, Dedication (SLM edition omits the last two lines: "By the Cinque Ports, | England. 1923." which appear in the Century edition); vii, Contents, verso [viii], blank; [1] divisional half-title· Changeling And Other Stories; verso [2], blank; 3–407, text. followed by single blank unnumbered page, flyleaf and verso, blank, and end paper. Not illustrated 7/6.

Binding: Bound in black cloth, with lettering in green as follows: *Backstrip:* Changeling | And · Other Stories | Donn Byrne | Sampson Low. Single green lines across backstrip, ½ cm. from top and lower edges. *Front cover:* Changeling | And Other Stories | Donn Byrne The whole enclosed in a rectangle formed by a single green line of same width as that on backstrip, inset ½ cm. from edges. Back cover blank; white end papers, all edges cut.

Reprinted, uniform edition, 1931 (April), 3/6; cheaper edition, 1931 (July), 2 6.

Reprint

New York: Grosset & Dunlap, 1931. "Novels of distinction" series. 20 ⁄ 14 cm. 418 p. Not illustrated. $1.00.

Contents: Changeling. The barnacle goose. Belfasters. The keeper of the bridge. In praise of Lady Margery Kyteler. Reynardine. Dramatis personae. Wisdom buildeth her house. The Parliament at Thebes. Delilah, now it was dusk. A quatrain of Ling Tai Fu's. "Irish." By ordeal of justice. A story against women.

The Century and Grosset & Dunlap editions omit "A story against women"; the Sampson Low edition omits "A quatrain of Ling Tai Fu's" and "By ordeal of justice."

First editions:

Century. There were two printings in 1923, with no established distinction. A personal communication from the Century Co. gives the date of the printing order for the first printing as August 20, 1923, and that for the second printing as December 7, 1923. It has been suggested that the first printing is that bound in vertical-ribbed cloth, with distance of 173 mm. between rules on spine, and the second, bound in smooth cloth, with a between-rules distance of 177 mm.; this has not been definitely proved to be the case.

Sampson Low. First printing bears no date; bound in black cloth, with green lettering.

Periodical publication:

Changeling. *Hearst's international,* 39:2, p. 15–17, 71ff.; 3, p. 44–46, 66ff.; 4, p. 34–35, 65ff.; February, March, April, 1921. Illustrated by Harry Townsend. Title: "The woman God changed."

The barnacle goose. *Saturday evening post,* 189:7, p. 14–15, 48ff.; August 12, 1916. Illustrated by Harvey Dunn.

Belfasters. *Hearst's international,* 37:5, p. 31–33, 73ff.; May, 1920. Illustrated by Walter Everett. Title: "And Zabad begat Ephlal."

The keeper of the bridge. *McClure's magazine,* 53:4, p. 6–8. 32ff.; April, 1921. Illustrated by J. D. Gleason.

CHANGELING, AND OTHER STORIES

In praise of Lady Margery Kyteler. *Pictorial review*, 24:10, p. 10–11, 32ff.; July, 1923. Illustrated by James H. Crank. Title: "In praise of Lady Margery."
Reynardine. *McClure's magazine*, 53:5, p. 15–18, 51; May, 1921. Illustrated by A. I. Keller.
Dramatis personae. *Scribner's*, 72:2, p. 147–153; August, 1922. Not illustrated.
Wisdom buildeth her house. *Century magazine*, 103:2, p. 161–175, December, 1921. Illustrated by C. B. Falls.
The Parliament at Thebes *Pictorial review*, 24:9, p. 8–9, 78ff., June, 1923. Illustrated by Robert Lawson.
Delilah, now it was dusk. *Hearst's international*, 43:4, p. 70–75, 129ff.; April, 1923. Illustrated by Wilfred Jones.
A quatrain of Ling Tai Fu's. *Red book*, 29:4, p. 744–755; August, 1917. Illustrated by Harvey Dunn. Reprinted in *Ellery Queen's mystery magazine*, 11: 54, p. 94–120; May, 1948.
"Irish." *Chicago Tribune*, Sunday magazine section, December 31, 1922, p. 8–11. Illustrated by Garrett Price.
By ordeal of justice. *Hearst's international*, 40:4, p. 10–12, 84ff.; October, 1921. Illustrated by G. Patrick Nelson.
A story against women. *Collier's*, 72:23, p. 5–6, 24ff.; December 8, 1923. Illustrated by W. H. D. Koerner.

Notes on the individual stories:

Changeling. The title in its magazine appearance was "The woman God changed." Of the two motion pictures which were based upon it, one bears this latter title, and the other was called "His captive woman." Details concerning these screen versions will be found under "Cinematizations."
Mr. Macauley devotes considerable space to this book, both in his biography (p. 99ff) and in his *Bookman* article (April, 1929, p. 154). In the latter he makes the statement that it is "vivid and dramatic, a blend of O. Henry and Somerset Maugham." Not all of the reviewers were as enthusiastic.

The barnacle goose. This story was reprinted in the *Cork Examiner* shortly after Mr. Byrne's death, and is the subject of the letter quoted by Mr. Macauley on p. 193 of his biography. It also appears in the School Reader edition of *Messer Marco Polo*. Mr. O'Brien's *Best short stories of 1916* gives it two stars on the annual Roll of Honor.
Many critics have commented on the amount of autobiography which appears in this story; as a matter of fact, except that the tale is about an Irishman who migrates to America and later returns to Ireland, and that the setting of the action is in south Armagh, there is nothing whatever in the characterization or plot which parallels the life of Donn Byrne.

Belfasters. Original title was "And Zabad begat Ephlal." The story is given one star in Mr. O'Brien's annual Roll of Honor.

The keeper of the bridge. Like "The barnacle goose," this story is reprinted in the School Reader edition of *Messer Marco Polo*. It is discussed at some length in Mr. Macauley's biography (p. 97, 102), and in many of the reviews. It is placed in Group II in the annual listing of the *O. Henry Memorial Award prize stories* (1921 volume), and given a star in the annual index of Mr. O'Brien's *Best short stories of 1921*.

In praise of Lady Margery Kyteler. At the suggestion of Mr. Arthur T. Vance, editor of the *Pictorial review* at that time, the title of this story was shortened to "In praise of Lady Margery" when it appeared in this magazine. The manuscript

DONN BYRNE BIBLIOGRAPHY

is in the possession of Mr. Albert Sperisen, the well-known San Francisco collector. Mr O'Brien gives it a single star in his 1923 index. The story was probably written in July, 1922, while Donn Byrne was at Greythorn, Dun Laoghaire.

Reynardine. Reprinted in the *Grand magazine* (London), December, 1928. The story is listed in Group I in the 1921 volume of the *O Henry Memorial Award prize stories*, and is mentioned briefly by Miss Blanche Colton Williams in her review of "The short story of 1921" for the *New York Evening Post literary review* (December 31, 1921).

Dramatis personae. Reprinted in the *Irish review*, December, 1922. Mr. O'Brien's 1922 anthology of *Best short stories* lists with single asterisk, indicating distinction, on Roll of Honor.

Wisdom buildeth her house. The manuscript of this story, in the Wetherbee Collection, bears the original title "The Arab lady," lined out, with a second title "Solomon called the wise," also lined out and the final title substituted. Dealing as it does with one of the author's favorite themes, it is generally conceded to be among the best of his short stories. It was written at Riverside "in a month's interlude between chapters of *Fiddler's Green (The Wind bloweth)*" probably in the summer of 1921.

The story received a great deal of critical comment, the most interesting of which is contained in the following references. "Among our contributors" column, *Century magazine*, December, 1921; April, 1922; May, 1922, *O. Henry Memorial Award prize stories of 1921*. Despite Mr. Macauley's statement that the story was reprinted in this anthology, such was not actually the case; it is, however, discussed at some length in the preface, *Best short stories of 1922* (single asterisk, indicating distinction, in annual Roll of Honor). "The short story of 1921," by Blanche Colton Williams in *New York Evening Post literary review*, December 31, 1921.

The Parliament at Thebes. This tale was also singled out for particular comment by many of the reviewers of *Changeling*, but most of the references are brief and uncritical. Mr. O'Brien gives it two asterisks in his 1923 volume.

Delilah, now it was dusk. Reprinted in *Dublin magazine*, 1:1, p. 7–16, August, 1923. Not illustrated. Given two asterisks in Mr. O'Brien's 1923 "Roll of Honor."

A quatrain of Ling Tai Fu's. The front cover of the *Red book* for August, 1917, announces this as "the most remarkable story Donn Byrne has written." Mr. Macauley comments: "Nearly as perfect an example of its kind as one could find ... somewhat suggestive of O. Henry in method and treatment." There are more than the usual number of textual variations and discrepancies between the first (magazine) printing, and the version as subsequently reprinted in *Changeling*. The author was offered $100.00 for the motion picture rights to this story; apparently, he did not accept the offer.

"Irish." This story also differs considerably in its book version as compared with the earlier magazine appearance. Two asterisks in Mr. O'Brien's 1923 "Roll of Honor."

By ordeal of justice. Written in June, 1918, possibly at Oak Bluffs, Martha's Vineyard, Mass.; the author received $675.00 for it Mr. O'Brien lists this story in his 1922 anthology, but does not accord it any particular distinction.

A story against women. Variously reprinted, as follows: *Everybody's magazine*, 54:3, p. 128–138, 177; March, 1926. Illustrated by Harry T. Fisk; *Famous story magazine*, 3:2, p. 230–236; May, 1926. Not illustrated; *"Hosses,"* edited by Charles W. Gray. New York: Holt, 1927, p. 91–124. Not illustrated.

BLIND RAFTERY

The author's own opinion of this story, as quoted in *Collier's magazine,* December 8, 1923, p. 38: "I think it's by far the best short story I've ever done." As this story did not appear in the Century Co. edition of *Changeling,* it is not mentioned in the reviews which appeared in the United States; many of the English reviews of the Sampson Low edition single it out for special and highly favorable comment. Listed in Group I in the 1923 edition of the *O. Henry Memorial Award prize stories;* given one asterisk in Mr. O'Brien's 1924 anthology, and three in that for 1926.

Reviews: New York Evening Post literary review, October 27, 1923, p. 193; *The Nation,* New York, v. 117, Dec. 5, 1923, p. 655 (Joseph Wood Krutch); *The Times literary supplement,* London, v. 23, Oct. 23, 1924, p. 670; *The Independent,* New York, v. 111, Nov. 24, 1923, p. 254 (Margaret Ladd Franklin); *The Bookman,* London, v. 67, Nov., 1924, p. 119; *New York Times,* Oct. 19, 1924, III, 12:5 (Filson Young).

BLIND RAFTERY
The Century Co., 1924 (September)

Blind Raftery | And | His Wife, Hilaria | By | Donn Byrne | Author of "Messer Marco Polo," "The Wind Bloweth," etc. | Illustrated by | John Richard Flanagan | [cut] | The Century Co. | New York and London

Collation: Narrow 12mo (19 × 11½ cm.). 175 p. End paper; flyleaf and verso blank; [i] half-title: Blind Raftery; [ii] blank; frontispiece, inset opposite title page; [iii] title page, as above. Lettering enclosed in rectangle formed by double black lines, of different thickness, with lighter inside; [iv] Copyright, 1924, by | The Century Co. | [rule] | Copyright, 1924, by | The Pictorial Review Company | Printed in U. S. A.; [v] List of illustrations; [vi] blank; [1], divisional half-title: Blind Raftery; verso [2], blank; 3–175, text; followed by three blank unnumbered pages; flyleaf and verso, blank; end paper. Cloth, $1.25; leather, $2.50.

Binding: In two bindings, as follows:

a. Terra cotta cloth, lettered in black: *Backstrip:* Blind | Raf- | tery | [ornament] | Donn | Byrne | The | Century | Co. Blind panel stamped above title; three blind panels stamped between author's and publisher's names; publisher's name in fifth panel. *Front cover:* Blind | Raftery | By | Donn | Byrne Single solid black line extends vertically from top to lower edge of front cover, to left of lettering and 2½ cm. from hinge. Back cover blank except for corresponding line. White end papers, all edges cut.

b. Black leather, lettering in gold on *backstrip* as follows: Blind | Raf- | tery | Donn | Byrne | The | Century | Co. Front and back covers blank except for blind stamped single lines forming rectangles inset ½cm. from edges. White end papers, all edges cut, top edges gilt.

The exact publication date has not been determined. The Century Co. give as dates of the first four printing orders June 10 and October 7, 1924; January 3 and June 19, 1925. Publication is announced in the Weekly Record Column of the *Publishers' weekly* for September 20, 1924, indicating release some time

[17]

during the preceding week. From the large number of newspaper announcements dated September 14, this seems a likely date.

Sampson Low, Marston & Co., Ltd., 1925 (March)

Blind Raftery | And | His Wife, Hilaria | By | Donn Byrne | Author of "Messer Marco Polo," "The | Wind Bloweth," etc. | London | Sampson Low, Marston & Co., Ltd.

Collation: Large 12mo (21 x 14 cm.). 124 p. End paper; flyleaf and verso blank; [i] half-title: Blind Raftery, [ii] blank; [iii] title page, as above; [iv] Printed in Great Britain by Purnell and Sons | Paulton, Somerset, England; 1–124, text; followed by blank flyleaf and verso, and end paper. Not illustrated. 5 .

Binding: Bound in dark green cloth, lettered in gold on *backstrip:* Blind | Raftery | Donn Byrne | (the whole enclosed in a gold rectangle formed by single lines, 2 x 4 cm.) Sampson Low   *Front cover:* Blind stamped Irish harp in center, enclosed in blind stamped rectangle formed by double lines, the outer of which is ¼ cm. from edges. Back cover blank. Top edges only are cut. White end papers. Printed on very heavy stiff paper. Dust wrapper gray, of extra-heavy material.

Reprinted, uniform edition, 1931 (April); cheaper editions, 1931 (July); 1935 (September), 2/6.

First editions:
Century. Perfect type, last line p. 109; perfect type, lower right hand corner, p. 138. The card index file of the Harvard College Library gives two additional points as being of possible value: over-all measurement of lettering on spine 170 mm., as contrasted with a measurement of 165 mm. in second issue; a period after the "Co." at foot of spine, missing in second issue. Both of these are probably correct. A few leather-bound copies were included in the first printing.
Sampson Low. First edition bears no date, and there is no statement as to the printing. Subsequent printings so state. Bound in dark green cloth, with gilt lettering; printed on extra-heavy paper.
Periodical publication: Pictorial review, 25:11, p. 5–11, 64–76; August, 1924. The magazine contains many more of the John Richard Flanagan illustrations than were included in the Century Co. volume; many of these are of exceptional merit.

The manuscript was sold at auction in New York on January 28, 1937, bringing $500.00. The American Art Association-Anderson Galleries catalogue (no. 4296) of that date contains a description of the manuscript, which is now in the Houghton Library of Harvard College. It contains what is for the author an unusually large number of changes and corrections; not included with the Harvard collection, but in the Wetherbee Collection, are half a dozen scraps of notepaper, old envelopes, etc., on which, along with golf scores and other miscellaneous memoranda, the author jotted down preliminary notes regarding the verse and text of the book.

No inscribed presentation copy has come to the attention of the writer.

O'MALLEY OF SHANGANAGH—AN UNTITLED STORY

Mr. Byrne's own comment on this book (*Bookman*, 61·6, p. 729; August, 1925): "A trifle too full of sentiment."

Reviews: New York Evening Post literary review, Sept 20, 1924, p. 3 (Warner Olivier); *Saturday review of literature*, v. 1, Dec. 6, 1924, p. 363; *The Bookman*, New York, v. 60, November, 1924, p. 342, *New York Times*, Sept. 21, 1924, III, 19:2, *Times literary supplement*, London, v. 24, April 9, 1925, p. 252, *New York Tribune*, Sept. 30, 1924 (F. F. Van de Water).

O'MALLEY OF SHANGANAGH
AN UNTITLED STORY

The Century Co., 1925 (March 14)

O'Malley | Of | Shanganagh | By | Donn Byrne | Author of "Messer Marco Polo," "The Wind Bloweth," | "Blind Raftery," etc. | Illustrated by | John Richard Flanagan | [cut] | The Century Co. | New York and London

Collation: Narrow 12mo (19 x 11½ cm.). 207 p. End paper; flyleaf and verso, blank; [i–ii] blank; [iii] half-title: O'Malley | Of | Shanganagh; [iv] blank; frontispiece inset, facing title page; [v] title page, as above, with lettering enclosed in rectangle formed by double lines differing in width, 13 x 7 cm.; [vi] Copyright, 1924, 1925, by | The Century Co. | Printed in U. S. A.; [vii] list of illustrations; verso [viii], blank; [1] divisional half-title; O'Malley Of Shanganagh; verso [2], blank; 3–207, text; followed by single blank page, flyleaf and verso blank, and end paper. Cloth, $1.25; leather, gilt top, $2.50.

Binding: There were two forms of the binding:

a. Terra cotta cloth, with black lettering, as follows: *Backstrip:* O'Malley | Of | Shanganagh | Donn | Byrne | The | Century Co. *Front cover:* O'Malley | Of | Shanganagh | By | Donn | Byrne   Solid black line vertical on front and back covers, from top to lower edges, 2 cm. from hinge. Backstrip blind stamped with three rectangles, 2 x 3 cm., between author's and publisher's names, and two 1½ cm. blind stamped squares at top and lower edges. White end papers; all edges cut.

b. Black leather, flexible, lettered in gold on *backstrip:* O'Malley | Of | Shanganagh | Donn | Byrne | The | Century | Co. Front and back covers blank except for single lines blind stamped, forming rectangles inset ½ cm. from edges. White end papers; all edges cut; top edges gilt.

Sampson Low, Marston & Co., Ltd., 1925 (September)

An | Untitled Story | By | Donn Byrne | Author of | "Messer Marco Polo," "The Wind Bloweth" | "Blind Raftery," etc. | London | Sampson Low, Marston & Co., Ltd.

Collation: Large 12mo (20½ x 14 cm.). 156 p. End paper; flyleaf and verso, blank; [i] half-title: An Untitled Story; [ii] blank; [iii] title page, as above; [iv] Printed in Great Britain by Purnell and Sons | Paulton, Somerset, England;

1–158, text; followed by blank flyleaf and verso, and end paper. Not illustrated. 7/6.

Binding: Bound in green cloth, lettered in gold on *backstrip:* An | Untitled | Story | Donn | Byrne (the whole enclosed in a rectangle 2 × 5 cm., formed by single gold lines) | Sampson Low   Front cover blank except for rectangle formed by double lines, blind stamped, inset ½ cm. from edges. Back cover blank. White end papers; top edges only are cut.

Reprinted, uniform edition, 1931 (March), 3/6; cheaper editions, 1931 (July), 1935 (November), 2/6.

First editions:
Century. The WNBA copies preceded the first regular trade edition by nine days (see below). Aside from these, of the two printings known to have been ordered in 1925, no points have been established which definitely differentiate them. Mr. Albert Sperisen, the well-known San Francisco bibliophile, has suggested that the distinguishing feature of the first printing may be a slight blurring or fuzziness of the letter "r," page 41, line 21, third word "over," and that in the second printing the kern of the letter shows a complete break. Supporting evidence for this contention is the fact that the WNBA copies show this blurring, but it has not been definitely determined whether the broken kern first appears in the second, third, or some subsequent printing Of the first trade edition, a few copies were bound in leather, with gilt tops.

The WNBA copies, mentioned above, refer to a lot of 200 copies of the first edition which were presented by The Century Company to the members and guests of the Women's National Book Association, at their annual dinner in 1925. These have tipped in a printed notice, with the following inscription: To the members and guests of | The Women's National Book Association | At their annual dinner | Hotel McAlpin | Thursday Evening, March 5, 1925 | Compliments of The Century Co.

These copies, as stated above, preceded the regular trade edition by nine days; they are the only ones which are definitely known to be part of the first printing, and finally, they represent the only advance issue of any of the books by this author.

Sampson Low. First edition bears no date, and no statement as to printing Subsequent printings so state (?).

Periodical publication: Appeared under the title "An untitled story" in the *Century magazine,* v. 109, p. 147–167, 339–356, 538–551, December, 1924 – February, 1925. Not illustrated.

The manuscript was sold at auction in New York November 11, 1937, and is described in the American Art Association-Anderson Galleries catalogue of that date. It brought $190.00 and was purchased by a Philadelphia dealer, who later sold it to a private collector.

The compiler has no knowledge of any existing inscribed presentation copies of either the American or the English editions of this book. It was in the spring of 1925 that Mr. Byrne made a trip to the Near East, and it is probable that he was there when the book appeared in America; in the fall of this year, when the English edition was published, he was variously at Dartmouth in Devonshire, Surrey, and probably Ireland.

This book did much to bring its author into disfavor with the Catholic Church; see John J. Downey, "Some objections to the novels of Donn Byrne," *The Catholic world,* 128:767, p. 566–570, February, 1929.

HANGMAN'S HOUSE

Announced in "The Weekly Record" column of the *Publishers' weekly*, March 21, 1925.

Reviews: Saturday review of literature, 1:796, May 30, 1925; *Bookman*, London, 69:410, p. 134, November, 1925; *New York Evening Post literary review*, March 28, 1925, p. 4 (Warner Olivier); *New York Herald Tribune books*, March 22, 1925, p. 5 (Margery Latimer), *Saturday review*, London, 140:3651, p. 450, October 17, 1925.

HANGMAN'S HOUSE
The Century Co., 1926 (March)

Hangman's | House | By | Donn Byrne | Author of "Messer Marco Polo," "O'Malley | of Shanganagh," "The Wind Bloweth," etc. | Illustrated by | John Richard Flanagan | [publisher's device] | The Century Co. | New York & London.

First printing March, 1926; second, April, 1926; third, April, 1926; fourth, May, 1926; fifth, June, 1926; sixth, July, 1926.

Collation: 12mo (19 x 13 cm.). xiii, 466 p. End paper; flyleaf and verso, blank; [i] half-title: Hangman's | House; verso [ii], blank; frontispiece inset, facing title page [iii] as above. Lettering on title page enclosed in a rectangle formed by double lines of unequal width, the heavier being the outer, 13½ x 8¼ cm.; [iv] Copyright, 1925, 1926, by | The Pictorial Review Company | Copyright, 1926, by | The Century Co. | [rule] | First printing, March, 1926 | Printed in U. S. A.; v–viii: A Foreword to Foreigners; xiii, list of illustrations; verso [xiv], blank; [1], divisional half-title: Hangman's House; verso [2], blank; 3–466, text; followed by blank flyleaf and verso, and end paper. $2.50.

Binding: Bound in terra cotta cloth, lettered in black as follows: *Backstrip:* Hang- | man's | House | [ornament] | Donn | Byrne | The | Century | Co. *Front cover:* Hangman's | House | By | Donn | Byrne   Solid black line vertically on front and back covers, extending from top to lower edge, 2½ cm. from hinge. White end papers; all edges cut. On backstrip are five blind stamped rectangles, one of which, 1 x 2½ cm., is above the title, three, 3 x 2½ cm., are between author's and publisher's names, and the fifth, 1½ x 2½ cm., contains publisher's name. Printer's decoration between title and author's name.

Limited edition: Rag paper, boards and quarter vellum; brown end papers and flyleaf; edges uncut; backstrip lettered in gold. Illustrated by John Richard Flanagan. $10.00. Inscribed: This large-paper edition of | Hangman's House | is limited to 350 copies | signed by the author | of which 345 are for sale | [signature] | This constitutes the first edition, | printed March, 1926.

Sampson Low, Marston & Co., Ltd., 1926 (March)

Hangman's | House | By | Donn Byrne | London | Sampson Low, Marston & Co., Ltd.

Collation: 12mo (19 x 13 cm.). x, 406 p. End paper; flyleaf and verso, blank; [i] half-title: Hangman's House; [ii] Other novels by Mr. Donn Byrne (list follows); [iii] title page, as above; [iv] Printed in Great Britain by Purnell and Sons Paulton, Somerset, England; v–x, A Foreword to Foreigners; [1] divisional half-title: Hangman's House; verso [2], blank; 3–406, text; followed by blank flyleaf and verso, and end paper. Not illustrated. 7/6.

Binding: Bound in black cloth, lettered as follows: Backstrip: Hangman's | House | Donn | Byrne | Sampson Low. Lettering is in gold, and single lines, also gold, extend across backstrip ½ cm. from top and lower edges. Front cover: Hangman's House | Donn Byrne. Blind stamped, and enclosed in a rectangle formed by single lines, also blind stamped, inset ½ cm. from edges. Back cover: Publisher's device blind stamped in lower right corner. White end papers; all edges cut.

Reprinted, uniform edition, 1931 (February); cheaper edition, 1931 (July), 3 6.

Reprints

New York: Grosset & Dunlap, 1928. "Novels of distinction" series. 20 × 14 cm. xiii, 466 p. Illustrated by John Richard Flanagan. $1.00. Also, Motion picture edition, illustrated with scenes from the William Fox-John Ford photoplay. 75 cents.

New York: Editions for the Armed Forces, Inc. Paper, 17 × 11½ cm. 320 p. Not illustrated. No date. No. N–21 in this series, established by the Council on Books in Wartime.

London: John Lane Co., 1936 (January). No. 24 in "Penguin books" series. Paper, 19 × 13 cm. 288 p. 6d. Reprinted in this edition August, 1936; March, 1937; November, 1937; August, 1939.

First editions:
Century: The Limited Edition. First trade edition: "First Printing, March, 1926." on copyright page.
Sampson Low. First edition bears no date, nor any statement as to printing. All subsequent printings so marked on p. [ii].
Periodical publication: The Pictorial review, New York, 27:2, p. 5–9, 42ff.; 3, p. 23–27, 64ff.; 4, p. 19–23, 68ff.; 5, p. 20–24, 129ff.; November, 1925 – February, 1926. Illustrated by John Richard Flanagan.
The story which comprises part 2 of chapter XVI was published separately in magazine form, under the title "The blue waves of Tory." See *Pictorial review,* 26:9, p. 8–9, 46ff.; June, 1925. Illustrated by John Richard Flanagan. Also printed in *Cornhill magazine,* 59:350, p. 174–183; August, 1925. Not illustrated.
This magazine version differs slightly from that which was subsequently included in the book; it is of some additional interest in that it introduces the character "Uncle Valentine" who later appears in the "Destiny Bay" stories. The "Kerry" of the "Destiny Bay" stories here bears the name of "Ronnie." The manuscript pages containing this material are in the Wetherbee Collection. Mr.

BROTHER SAUL

O'Brien gives this story three stars, indicating distinction, in his 1925 "Roll of Honor."

The manuscript was sold at auction in New York in 1937; it is now in the possession of the Harvard College Library.

In a letter to Mr. John Ford, who directed the William Fox motion picture production, Donn Byrne wrote: "The writing of this novel gave me the greatest satisfaction of my literary career. I hope you will find equal pleasure in filming it."

A number of writers of general articles about Donn Byrne have singled out *Hangman's House* for particular mention. See, especially, in General Reference List, Mr. Lucas' *Reading, writing, and remembering*, Mr. Dickinson's *Best books of the decade 1926–1935*, and Mr. Townsend's *Good reading*.

Mr. Macauley's biography (p. 109ff.) also devotes considerable critical comment to this particular book, and (p 118–120) quotes at some length from the letter in which the author defends himself and his novel against objections on the part of "a New York critic and a correspondent of The Chicago Tribune."

Reviews: Saturday review of literature, 2:807, May 22, 1926 (Grace Frank); Bookman, New York, 63:4, p. 481, June, 1926 (Frances Newman); *New York Times*, III, 8:2, May 9, 1926; *New York Herald Tribune books*, May 2, 1926, p. 6 (Mary Ross); *New York Evening Post literary review*, April 24, 1926 (W. O. Tewson); *Bookman*, London, 70:415, p. 52, April, 1926 (Mary Webb); *New York World*, May 19, 1926, p. 15 (Heywood Broun).

BROTHER SAUL

The Century Co., 1927 (April 15)

Brother Saul | Donn Byrne | [publisher's device] | The Century Co. | New York & London

Collation: 12mo (19 x 13 cm.). 487 p. End paper; flyleaf and verso blank; [i–iv] blank; [v] half-title: Brother Saul; [vi] blank; [vii] title page, as above. Lettering enclosed in a rectangle 14½ x 9 cm., formed by double black lines of unequal width, the thicker being outside; [viii] Copyright, 1926, 1927, by | The Pictorial Review Company | Copyright, 1927, by | The Century Co. | [rule] | First printing, April, 1927 | Second printing, April, 1927 | Printed in U. S. A.; [ix] Dominam Amicamque | Ad | Dorotheam; [x] blank; [xi], six-line paraphrase of a Cornish child's prayer; verso [xii], blank; [xiii] Author's note, verso [xiv], blank; [1], divisional half-title: Brother Saul; [2] inscription and translation of inscription on apse of an old church in Byzantium; 3–487, text, followed by three blank pages, blank flyleaf and verso, and end paper. Not illustrated. $2.50.

Third printing, May, 1927.

Binding: Bound in terra cotta cloth, lettered in black as follows: *Backstrip*: Brother | Saul | [ornament] | Donn | Byrne | The | Century | Co. Blind stamped rectangle 1 x 2 cm. above title; three, 2 x 3 cm., between author's and publisher's names; one, 1½ x 2 cm., containing publisher's name. *Front cover*: Brother | Saul | By | Donn | Byrne On front and back covers, a single black line extends vertically from top to lower edge, 2½ cm. from hinge. White end papers; all edges cut.

The Limited Edition, 21 × 14½ cm., is bound in boards and vellum, with vellum corners; brown end papers and flyleaves; uncut, large rag paper. Not illustrated. $10.00.

Sampson Low, Marston & Co., Ltd., 1927 (April 4)

Brother Saul | By | Donn Byrne | London | Sampson Low, Marston & Co., Ltd.

Collation: 12mo (19 × 13 cm.). 476 p. End paper; flyleaf and verso, blank; [I] half-title: Brother Saul, [II] Other Novels by Mr. Donn Byrne (list follows); [III] title page, as above; [iv] Printed in Great Britain by Purnell and Sons | Paulton, Somerset, England; [v] inscription, with translation, on apse of an old church in Byzantium; [vI] Author's note; [vII] Dominam Amicamque | Ad | Dorotheam; [vIII] six-line paraphrase of a Cornish child's prayer; 1–[476], text; followed by blank flyleaf and verso, and end paper. Not illustrated. 7/6.

Uniform edition, 1931 (February); cheaper editions, 1931 (March, July), 3/6; 1938 (May), 6d.

Binding. Bound in black cloth, lettered as follows· *Backstrip:* Brother | Saul | Donn ' Byrne   Sampson Low (in gold). *Front cover·* Brother Saul | Donn Byrne (blind stamped, the whole enclosed in a rectangle, blind stamped, inset 1½ cm. from edges). Back cover blank except for publisher's device blind stamped in lower right corner. White end papers, all edges cut.

Reprint

New York: Grosset & Dunlap, 1930. "Novels of distinction" series. 20 × 14 cm. 487 p. Not illustrated. $1.00.

First editions:
Century The limited edition bears the following inscription: This large-paper edition of | Brother Saul | is limited to 500 copies | signed by the author | of which 495 are for sale | (signature) | This constitutes the first edition, | printed April, 1927. On copyright page is legend "First printing, April, 1927." The first trade edition bears the statement, on copyright page, "Second printing, April, 1927."

Sampson Low. First printing bears no date, nor any statement as to printing. Subsequent printings so state (?).

Periodical publication: The Pictorial review, 28:3, p. 8–11, 31ff.; 4, p. 14–16, 57ff; 5, p. 21–25, 104ff.; 6, p. 24–25, 110ff.; 7, p. 24–25, 108ff.; 8, p. 26, 60ff.; December, 1926 – May, 1927. Illustrated by E. F. Ward.

There are a great many variations and discrepancies between the magazine and book versions, and various differences between the manuscript text and that of the printed appearance.

In addition to many differences in punctuation, in phrasing, paragraph arrangement, and certain omissions and additions, the magazine version omits the dedication and the three introductory notes which appear in the Century

CRUSADE

and Sampson Low volumes, and omits also that part of the text which comprises p. 442-end in the Century edition.

The manuscript of *Brother Saul*, formerly in the possession of Mr. Benjamin D. Hitz, the Indianapolis bibliophile, is now part of the Byrne collection in the Harvard College Library. Single pages of the manuscript are reproduced in the Sampson Low edition of Mr. Macauley's biography, and in Mr. Malone's *Donn Byrne, an Irish realist*. In the Wetherbee Collection are the holograph sheets and corrected page-proofs of the dedication to Mrs. Donn Byrne, the inscription on the Byzantine church, the Cornish child's prayer, and the Author's Note.

The following inscribed presentation copies are known:

a. Sampson Low first edition inscribed to Shane Leslie: "Do mo caraid | Sean Leslie | O Brian na Beirne-donn , 'Donn Byrne' " | This copy was sold at auction by the Parke-Bernet Galleries, March 3, 1938, later it came into the possession of Mr. Hitz of Indianapolis, and is now part of the Donn Byrne collection at the Harvard College Library.

b. Sampson Low copy inscribed to Mrs. Donn Byrne: "Dolly | from Brian | April 4, 1927 | Donn Byrne" Inscription is on page opposite title page, which bears the following, printed in red ink: "This copy is unique in so far as it is the first completed copy of 'Brother Saul,' and is the only one printed on handmade paper." (In the Wetherbee Collection.)

Reviews: *Bookman*, London, 72:429, p. 192–193, June, 1927 (Cranstoun Metcalfe); *Saturday review of literature*, 3:802, May 7, 1927 (John Haynes Holmes); *New York World*, April 24, 1927, p. 10M (H. H. Powell); *Homiletic review*, 95:2, p. 116–118, February, 1928 (J. M. Dawson); *The Spectator*, 138:698, April 16, 1927; *Times literary supplement*, London, 26.296, April 28, 1927; *The Sphere*, London, 109:1424, p. 227, May 7, 1927 (Arnold Palmer); *The Christian century*, 44:28, p. 855, July 14, 1927 (Winifred E. Garrison); *New York Times*, III, 17:1, April 17, 1927; *The Churchman*, 136:12, p. 21, Sept. 17, 1927 (Scott Easton); *New York Evening Post literary review*, April 30, 1927, p. 9 (Frederick H. Martens).

CRUSADE

Little, Brown & Co., 1928 (March 10)

[Decoration] | Crusade (in red letters) | By Donn Byrne | [publisher's device] | Published in Boston by | Little, Brown, and Company | MCMXXVIII (Publisher's name also in red.)

Collation: 12mo (19½ x 14 cm.). 250 p. End paper and flyleaf, decorated by Henry Pitz; verso blank; [i–ii] blank; [iii] half-title: Crusade; [iv] blank; [v] title page, as above; [vi] Copyright, 1927, 1928, | By Donn Byrne | [rule] | All rights reserved | Published March, 1928 | Printed in the United States of America; [1] divisional half-title: Crusade; verso [2], blank; [3]–250, text; followed by two blank pages, blank verso of flyleaf, and decorated flyleaf and end paper. Not illustrated. $2.00.

Reprinted, March, 1928.

Binding: Bound in green cloth, lettered in black, as follows: *Backstrip:* Crusade | [small Maltese cross, red] | Donn | Byrne | Little, Brown | and

[25]

Company   *Front cover.* Crusade | Donn Byrne   Below lettering is device consisting of a red Maltese cross, 2½ x 2½ cm., on a black shield, surrounded by a single black line. Back cover blank, decorated pictorial end papers; top edges stained scarlet, all edges cut.

Limited Edition is bound in light violet cloth and quarter vellum; red Maltese cross on white shield on front cover; white end papers; top edges gilt; fore edges uncut. Not illustrated. $10.00.

Sampson Low, Marston & Co., Ltd., 1928 (February)

Crusade | By | Donn Byrne | London | Sampson Low, Marston & Co., Ltd.

Collation: 12mo (19 x 13 cm.). 240 p. End paper; flyleaf and verso, blank; [i] blank; [ii] Novels by Mr. Donn Byrne (list follows); [iii] half-title: Crusade; [iv], blank; [v] title page, as above; [vi] First published 1928 | Printed in Great Britain by Purnell and Sons | Paulton (Somerset) and London; 1–240, text; [241] An advertisement of | Mr. Donn Byrne's Novels; [242] blank; followed by eight unnumbered pages of advertisements, blank flyleaf and verso, and end paper. Not illustrated. 7/6.

Binding: Bound in black cloth, lettered as follows: *Backstrip:* (in gold) Crusade | Donn | Byrne | Sampson Low   Single gold lines across backstrip, ½ cm. from top and lower edges. *Front cover:* (blind stamped) Crusade | Donn Byrne   Blind stamped single-line rectangle inset ½ cm. from edges. White end papers; all edges cut.

Uniform edition, 1931 (February), 6/; cheaper edition, 1931 (July), 3/6.

First editions:

Little, Brown. The limited edition bears the following inscription: Three hundred and sixty-five copies of this Limited | Edition have been printed, and are inscribed by the | Author. Of the three hundred and fifty copies | which are for sale | this is Copy . . . . . | (signature). First trade edition, "Published March, 1928" on copyright page.

Sampson Low. "First published, 1928" on verso of title page.

Periodical publication: Saturday evening post, 200:13, p. 3–5, 114ff.; 14, p. 20–21, 72ff.; 15, p. 32–33, 169ff.; 16, p. 32–33, 187ff.; September 24, October 1, 8, 15, 1927. Illustrated by F. R. Gruger.

The manuscript was sold by the Hoosier Bookshop, Indianapolis, in 1940, and is described in their catalogue no. 80 of that year. It is now part of the Donn Byrne collection in the Harvard College Library.

A condensed version of the book appeared in *The World review* (Mt. Morris, Ill.), 7:6–7, 29; September 17 and 24, 1928.

No inscribed presentation copies of this book are known to the present writer.

Reviews: New York Herald Tribune books, March 18, 1928, p. 3 (Frederick H. Martens); *Bookman,* London, 74:439, p. 60, April, 1928; *Saturday review of literature,* 4:38, p. 760, April 14, 1928 (Robert B. Macdougall); *The Spectator,* 140:329, March 3, 1928 (Rachel A. Taylor); *New York Times,* IV, 8:5, March 18, 1928; *Harper's magazine,* 156:936, May, 1928 (Harry Hansen); *Times literary*

DESTINY BAY

supplement, London, 27:128, Feb. 23, 1928; *Manchester guardian*, March 23, 1928 (R. B. L.); *The Nation*, 126:494, April 25, 1928 (Clifton Fadiman); *New republic*, 54:279, April 18, 1928 (C. A. C.); *New York Evening Post*, March 31, 1928, p. 12 (Ray C. B. Brown); *Bookman*, New York, 67:4, p. 464, June, 1928.

DESTINY BAY

Little, Brown & Co., 1928 (September 6)

Destiny | Bay | By Donn Byrne | Boston [publisher's device] 1928 | Little, Brown, and Company

Collation: 12mo (20 x 14 cm.). 350 p. End paper; flyleaf and verso blank; [i–ii] blank; [iii] half-title: Destiny Bay | [rule] |; [iv] By Donn Byrne | Crusade | Destiny Bay, the whole enclosed in a single-line rectangle 3 x 5 cm.; [v] title page, as above; lettering enclosed in a rectangle 14 x 8½ cm., formed by green decorative double line; [vi] Copyright, 1925, 1926, 1928, | By Estate of Brian Oswald Donn Byrne | [rule] | All rights reserved | Published September, 1928 | Printed in the United States of America; [vii] dedication; [viii] author's statement; [ix] Contents; [x] blank; [1] divisional half-title: One | [rule] | Tale of my Cousin Jenico at | Spanish Men's Rest; [2] blank; [3]–350, text; followed by blank flyleaf and verso, and end paper. Not illustrated. $2.50.

Binding: Bound in jade green cloth, with lettering in gold, as follows: *Backstrip:* Destiny | Bay | [small Irish harp] | Donn | Byrne | Little, Brown | and Company   *Front cover:* Destiny Bay | Donn Byrne | [two Irish harps, similar to, but slightly larger than that on backstrip]. Back cover blank; orange end papers and flyleaves; fore edges and lower edges uncut; top edges stained orange.

The Limited Edition is bound in Nile green cloth, with quarter vellum and vellum-tipped corners, frontispiece (portrait of author) faces title page; top edges are gilt, fore edges, and lower edges uncut. White end papers. $10.00.

Through courtesy of Messrs. Little, Brown and Company, it is possible to furnish the following list of printings, which is complete through June, 1938: September, 1928 (two printings); October, 1928; November, 1928; December, 1928; February, 1929; July, 1929; October, 1929; January, 1930; December, 1930; November, 1932; March, 1934; December, 1935; July, 1937.

Sampson Low, Marston & Co., Ltd., 1928 (September)

Destiny Bay | By | Donn Byrne | London | Sampson Low, Marston & Co., Ltd.

Collation: 12mo (19 x 13½ cm.). vii, 432 p. End paper; flyleaf and verso, blank; [i] half-title: Destiny Bay; [ii] Other Novels by Mr. Donn Byrne (list follows); [iii] title page, as above; [iv] First published . . . 1928 | Printed in Great Britain by Purnell and Sons | Paulton (Somerset) and London; [v] dedication; [vi] author's statement; vii, Contents; verso [viii], blank; 1–432, text; followed by sixteen unnumbered pages of advertisements, blank flyleaf and verso, and end paper. Not illustrated. 7/6.

Binding: Bound in black cloth, lettered as follows: *Backstrip:* (in gold) Destiny | Bay | Donn | Byrne | Sampson Low   Single lines across backstrip, ½ cm.

[27]

from top and lower edges. *Front cover:* (blind stamped) Destiny Bay | Donn Byrne   The whole enclosed in a rectangle formed by single lines inset ½ cm. from edges. Back cover blank except for publisher's device blind stamped in lower right hand corner; white end papers; all edges cut.

Uniform edition, 1931 (April), 6/; cheaper edition, 1931 (July), 3/6; new edition (paper), 256 p, 1938 (March), 6d.

Reprint

Garden City, N. Y.: The Sun Dial Press, 1942 (May 4). Reprint, from original plates. 79 cents.

Contents. Tale of my cousin Jenico at Spanish Men's Rest. Tale of my aunt Jenepher's wooing. Tale of James Carabine. Tale of the piper. Tale of my uncle Cosimo and the fair girl of Wu. Tale of Golfer Gilligan. Tale of the gypsy horse. Tale of Kerry. Tale told in Destiny Bay.

First editions:

Little, Brown. The limited edition has inscription: Three hundred and sixty-five copies of | this Limited Edition have been printed. | Of the three hundred and fifty copies | which are for sale | this is Copy . . . . . Trade edition, on copyright page: Published September, 1928.

Sampson Low. On verso of title page. First published . . . 1928.

The manuscript of *Destiny Bay* forms part of the Donn Byrne collection in the Harvard College Library. It is described as being in 546 quarto pages, signed in thirteen places. It is of peculiar interest in that it contains a tenth "Destiny Bay" story, entitled "The meditations of Kerry MacFarlane," which neither appears in the printed volume, nor was ever published elsewhere. It is not properly a story in itself, but rather a sort of prefatory sketch, which ties together a little more closely the several rather unconnected tales which comprise the book.

A reproduction of a single page of the manuscript (from the "Tale of the gypsy horse") illustrates the Sampson Low edition of Mr. Macauley's biography (p. 116f.), and also Mr. Malone's *Donn Byrne, an Irish realist* (p. 7).

As this volume was not published until after the author's death, no inscribed presentation copies exist. The only association items in this category are four copies of the book, on rag paper and in special morocco binding, which were made for each of Mr. Byrne's children; the individual recipient's name is indicated on each copy. It will be remembered that this volume is dedicated to the children, and that the dedication is known to have been one of the last things written by Mr. Byrne.

In a letter written to Miss Blanche Colton Williams, October 20, 1926, from Warren Farm House, Donn Byrne writes in part as follows: " . . . a book to be called Destiny Bay to be published next year. It is the history of an Irish family written in several parts with long poems in between and is a special child of my heart." As the manuscript contains no poems, it must be assumed that Donn Byrne gave up the idea of writing them, and used the short short stories instead.

IRELAND, THE ROCK WHENCE I WAS HEWN

Notes on the individual stories:

Tale of my cousin Jenico at Spanish Men's Rest. *Saturday evening post*, 198:15, p. 3–5, 146ff.; 16, p. 30–31, 159ff.; October 10, 17, 1925. Illustrated by F. R. Gruger. Magazine title: "Spanish Men's Rest."

Tale of my aunt Jenepher's wooing. *Pictorial review*, 26:10, p. 5–7, 90ff.; July, 1925. Illustrated by John Richard Flanagan. Magazine title: "County people." This story was given one asterisk, indicating distinction, in Mr. O'Brien's 1925 anthology of Best Short Stories.

Tale of James Carabine. *Saturday evening post*, 197:45, p. 3–5, 133ff; May 9, 1925. Illustrated by F. R. Gruger. Magazine title: "In praise of James Carabine." Original manuscript title was "James Carabine's last fight." This story has been made into a motion picture, and has also appeared in several anthologies. Details concerning these will be found under the appropriate section in subsequent pages.

Tale of the piper. No magazine publication prior to appearance in book form, but was subsequently reprinted in the *Golden book magazine* (19:112, p. 435–437; April, 1934. Illustrated by J. Burlin). Mr. O'Brien gives this story a single asterisk in his 1935 anthology.

Tale of my uncle Cosimo and the fair girl of Wu. *Pictorial review*, 26:7, p. 14–16, 60ff.; April, 1925. Illustrated by John Richard Flanagan. Magazine title "The fair girl of Wu." Reprinted in *Grand magazine* (London), July, 1929, under title "The fair girl of Wu." Original title in manuscript was "Tale of the Chinese woman." Single asterisk in Mr. O'Brien's 1925 anthology.

Tale of Golfer Gilligan. No magazine appearance prior or subsequent to publication in book. Manuscript title was "Tale of the Golfer Gilligan."

Tale of the gypsy horse. *Saturday evening post*, 199:15, p. 3, 226ff., 16, p. 28–29, 149ff.; October 9, 16, 1926. Illustrated by F. R. Gruger. Magazine title: "The Derby rule." See under "Anthologies."

Tale of Kerry. *Pictorial review*, 27:10, p. 7–9, 40ff; July, 1926. Illustrated by John Richard Flanagan. Magazine title "The wall that is high." Given listing in Group I in the 1926 edition of the *O. Henry Memorial Award prize stories*; two asterisks in the 1926 Best Short Stories anthology.

Tale told in Destiny Bay. No magazine publication.

Reviews: New York Herald Tribune books, Sept. 9, 1928, p. 5 (Herschel Brickell); *Saturday review of literature*, 5:141, Sept. 22, 1928 (Thurston Macauley); *New York Times*, IV, 6:4, Sept. 16, 1928; *Outlook*, New York, 150: 956, Oct. 10, 1928; *Spectator*, London, 141:340, Sept. 15, 1928 (R. A. Taylor); *Bookman*, London, 75:446, p. 124, November, 1928 (Cranstoun Metcalfe); *Correspondant*, Paris, Jan. 10, 1932, p. 138–146 (André Bellesort); *Quarterly review*, London, 251:498, p. 413, October, 1928; *New York Sun*, Sept. 17, 1928, p. 22; *Times literary supplement*, London, 27:706, Oct. 4, 1928.

IRELAND, THE ROCK WHENCE I WAS HEWN
Little, Brown & Co., 1929 (July 8)

Donn Byrne | Ireland | The Rock | Whence I Was Hewn | Foreword by the | Right Honourable T. P. O'Connor | With Illustrations | Little, Brown, and Company | Boston 1929

Collation: 8vo (22½ × 15½ cm.). 146 p. End paper; flyleaf and verso, blank; [i–ii] blank; [iii] half-title: Ireland | The Rock Whence I was Hewn; [iv] By

Donn Byrne   Crusade | Destiny Bay | Ireland: | The Rock Whence I was Hewn   The whole enclosed in a single-line rectangle, 4 x 6 cm.; [v] blank; [vi] frontispiece (map), [vii] title page, as above, with triple wavy rules at top and bottom; [viii] [triple wavy rules] | Copyright, 1927, | By National Geographic Society | Copyright, 1929, By Dorothea Donn-Byrne | [triple wavy rules] | All rights reserved | Published July, 1929 | Printed in the United States of America; [ix] acknowledgment to N. G. S., [x] blank; [xi–xii] illustration list; [1] Foreword | By The Right Honourable T. P. O'Connor; verso [2], blank; 3–18, text of Foreword; [19] divisional half-title: Ireland | The Rock Whence I Was Hewn; [20] blank; 21–146, text; followed by two blank pages, blank flyleaf and verso, and end paper. Illustrated. $2.50.

Binding: Bound in jade green cloth, lettered in gold, as follows: *Backstrip:* Donn | Byrne | Ireland | The | Rock | Whence | I | Was | Hewn | Little, | Brown | And | Company   *Front cover:* Donn | Byrne | Ireland | The Rock Whence I Was Hewn   Back cover blank; small shamrocks, black, on backstrip, above author's name and below publisher's name. Triple black line separates title from author's name. On front cover, six rows of similar shamrocks, also in black, form a diamond-shaped decorative pattern. White end papers; top edges stained orange; fore edges uncut.

Sampson Low, Marston & Co., Ltd., 1929 (Feb. 19)

Ireland | The Rock whence I was Hewn | Donn Byrne | Author of "Destiny Bay," "Hangman's House," etc. | Foreword | By the Right Hon. T. P. O'Connor | London | Sampson Low, Marston and Co., Ltd.

Collation: 12mo (19 x 13½ cm.). xxi, 104 p. End paper; flyleaf and verso, blank; [i] half-title: Ireland | The Rock whence I was Hewn; [ii] Other Novels by Mr. Donn Byrne (list follows); frontispiece inset opposite title page [iii], as above. Lettering of title page enclosed in rectangle 11 x 7 cm., formed by fine black line decorative border; [iv] Made and printed in Great Britain by Purnell and Sons   Paulton (Somerset) and London; [v] acknowledgment to N. G. S.; [vi] blank; vii–xxi, Foreword; [xxii] blank; [xxiii] divisional half-title: Ireland | The Rock whence I was Hewn; [xxiv] blank; 1–104, text; followed by eight unnumbered pages of advertisements, blank flyleaf and verso, and end paper. Illustrated. 5/.

Binding: Bound in black cloth, with lettering as follows: *Backstrip.* (in gold) Ireland | The Rock | Whence | I Was Hewn | Donn Byrne | Sampson Low   *Front cover:* (blind stamped) Ireland | The Rock Whence I Was Hewn | Donn Byrne (the whole enclosed in a single-line rectangle inset ½ cm. from edges). Back cover blank; white end papers; all edges cut.

Reprinted, uniform edition, 1931 (April); cheaper edition, 1931 (July), 3/6.

First editions:
Little, Brown. On copyright page, "Published July, 1929."
Sampson Low. No date; no statement as to printing. Subsequent editions so state.

FIELD OF HONOR—THE POWER OF THE DOG

Periodical appearance: National geographic magazine, v. 51, p. 257–326, March, 1927. With 68 illustrations in black-and-white, 11 illustrations in color, and 1 page map.

The number of illustrations differs in each of the three published editions. The *National geographic magazine* contains eighty (including the map), the Sampson Low volume forty-six, and the Little, Brown edition twenty-four. The *National geographic magazine* omits the Foreword by the Honourable T. P. O'Connor.

The manuscript of this work was sold at auction in New York on February 25, 1938, and is described in the Parke-Bernet Galleries catalogue no. 11, of that date.

An article by Ishbel Ross entitled "Geography, Inc." which appeared in *Scribner's magazine*, June, 1938 (103:6, p. 23–27, 57) refers to Donn Byrne as one of the "literary figures of the first water" who have contributed to the *National geographic magazine*.

Reviews: New York Times, IV, 11:2, July 21, 1929; *Saturday review of literature*, 6:24, Aug. 3, 1929 (D. C. Russell); *New York Herald Tribune books*, June 30, 1929, p. 7 (Norah Meade); *Bookman*, London, 76:452, p. 131, May, 1929 (Shan Bullock); *Times literary supplement*, London, 28:210, March 14, 1929; *New York Sun*, Nov. 2, 1929 (D. J. Marshall).

FIELD OF HONOR
THE POWER OF THE DOG

The Century Co., 1929 (September 6)

[Ornament] | Field of | Honor | By | Donn Byrne | Author of "Messer Marco Polo" | "Hangman's House" | "Brother Saul," etc. | The Century Co. | New York & London.

Collation: 12mo (19½ x 13½ cm.). 435 p. End paper; flyleaf and verso, blank; [i–ii] blank; [iii] half-title: Field of Honor; [iv] blank; [v] title page, as above. The whole enclosed in a rectangle 14½ x 9 cm., composed of an outer heavy black line, an inner row of small six-pointed stars, with a narrow black line between the two; [vi] Copyright, 1929, by | The Pictorial Review Company | Copyright, 1929, by | The Century Co. | First printing July, 1929 | Printed in U. S. A.; [vii] quotation from the Office of Compline on Passion Sunday; [viii] blank; [1] divisional half-title: Part I; verso [2], blank; 3–435, text; followed by five blank pages, blank flyleaf and verso, and end paper. Not illustrated. $2.50.

Binding: Bound in terra cotta cloth, with lettering in black as follows: *Backstrip:* Field | Of | Honor | [ornament (shamrock)] | Donn | Byrne | The | Century | Co. Five blind stamped panels, one above title, three between author's and publisher's names, and fifth containing publisher's name. *Front cover:* Field | Of | Honor | By | Donn Byrne   Solid black line extends vertically along front and back covers, 2½ cm. from backstrip, from top to lower edge. White end papers; all edges cut.

First printing, July, 1929; second printing, July, 1929; third printing, September, 1929; fourth printing, November, 1929.

[31]

The Limited Edition, 21½ × 15 cm., is on large rag paper, bound in boards and quarter vellum; brown end papers; top and fore edges uncut. Inscription: This large-paper edition of | Field of Honor | is limited to 500 copies | of which 493 are for sale | [signed by Dorothea Donn-Byrne as Literary Executrix]. Not illustrated. $10.00. Publisher's description: 21 × 33 picas, 435 pages, 10 Caslon no. 2, Rex no. 4 pattern, 500 copies on no. 66 Lindenmeyer. No statement as to date of printing.

Sampson Low, Marston & Co., Ltd., 1929 (September)

The Power of | The Dog | By | Donn Byrne | London | Sampson Low, Marston & Co., Ltd.

Collation: 12mo (19 × 13½ cm.). 473 p. End paper; flyleaf and verso, blank; [i] half-title: The Power of the Dog; [ii] Other Novels by Mr. Donn Byrne | [rule] | (list follows) | First Printed September, 1929, [iii] title page, as above; [iv] Made and printed in Great Britain by | Purnell and Sons, Paulton (Somerset) and London; [v] quotation from Office of Compline on Passion Sunday; verso [vi], blank; [1] Part I; verso [2], blank; 3–473, text; followed by blank page, flyleaf and verso, blank, and end paper. Not illustrated. 7/6.

Binding: Bound in black cloth, lettered as follows: *Backstrip:* (in gold) The Power | Of The | Dog | Donn | Byrne | Sampson Low   Single lines across backstrip, 1½ cm. from top and lower edges. *Front cover:* (blind stamped) The Power | Of The Dog | Donn Byrne   Back cover blank; white end papers; all edges cut.

The Limited Edition is on large rag paper, bound in green cloth and quarter vellum; top edges gilt; fore edges uncut; frontispiece (portrait of author over facsimile signature), facing title page. Inscription: Limited Edition | 516 copies | Of these 500 only are for sale | Of which this is number ... No statement as to date of printing. 42/.

Reprinted, uniform edition, 1931 (February), 6/; cheaper edition, 1931 (March, July), 3/6.

Reprint

New York: Grosset & Dunlap, 1931. "Novels of distinction" series. Cloth, 20 × 14 cm. 435 p. Not illustrated. $1.00.

First editions:

Century. The limited edition. First trade edition, on copyright page: First printing. July, 1929. (Not released for sale until September 6th.) "First printing" label on dust wrapper.

Sampson Low. The limited edition. First trade edition: "First printed, September, 1929" opposite title page.

Periodical publication: Pictorial review, 30:8, p. 9–13, 104ff.; 9, p. 16–20, 88ff.; 10, p. 20–24, 75ff.; 11, p. 23–29, 51ff.; May – August, 1929. Illustrated by Douglas Duer.

A PARTY OF BACCARAT—THE GOLDEN GOAT

The manuscript was sold at auction in New York on November 11, 1937, and is described in the American Art Association-Anderson Galleries catalogue no. 4346 of that date. This catalogue contains also a facsimile reproduction of a page from the manuscript; another page of the manuscript is reproduced in the Century Co. edition of Mr. Macauley's biography, opposite p. 88. This manuscript is now part of the Byrne collection of the Harvard College Library.

Projected titles for this book, in addition to the two actually used, included "The famous victory" (see Macauley, p. 188, Century), and "The lion and the unicorn" (see manuscript).

In the "blurb" accompanying the first installment of "Field of honor" in the *Pictorial review*, the following statement occurs: "Accompanying the manuscript was a letter in which Mr. Byrne stated 'I consider "Field of Honor" the finest story I have ever written.'"

Reviews: *Saturday review of literature*, 6:608, Dec. 28, 1929; *New York Times*, IV, 5:1, Sept. 15, 1929 (Louise Maunsell Field); *New York Evening Post*, Sept. 21, 1929, p. 6M (Vincent G. Byers); *Boston Evening Transcript*, Sept. 14, 1929, p. 3 (Sherwin L. Cook); *Bookman*, London, 77:457, p. 15, October, 1929 (Gregory Macdonald); *New York Herald Tribune books*, Sept. 8, 1929 (William McFee); *New York Evening Post*, Sept. 21, 1929, p. 7M (F. F. Van de Water); *Times literary supplement*, London, 28:1446, p. 816, Oct. 17, 1929; *Spectator*, London, no. 5282, p. 383, Sept. 21, 1929 (V. S. Pritchett).

A PARTY OF BACCARAT
THE GOLDEN GOAT
The Century Co., 1930 (April 11)

A Party of | Baccarat | By Donn Byrne | Illustrated by | Arthur William Brown | [publisher's device] | The Century Co. | New York   London.

Collation: Narrow 12mo (19 x 11½ cm.). x, 212 p. End paper; flyleaf and verso, blank; [i] half-title: A Party of Baccarat; verso [ii], Other Novels by Mr. Donn Byrne | [rule] | (list follows); frontispiece inset, facing title page; [iii] title page, as above. Decorative lines at top and bottom, above and below "Baccarat," and above and below "The Century Co."; [iv] copyright statement; First Printing | Printed in U. S. A.; v–x, Prologue; [xi] Illustrations; verso [xii], blank; [1] divisional half-title: A Party of Baccarat; verso [2], blank; 3–212, text, followed by blank flyleaf and verso, and end paper. Cloth, $1.25; leather, $2.50.

Binding: Bound in terra cotta cloth, lettered in black as follows: *Backstrip:* A | Party | Of | Baccarat | [ornament] | Donn | Byrne | The | Century | Co. *Front cover:* A | Party | Of | Baccarat | By | Donn | Byrne Single black line vertical on front and back covers, from top to lower edge, 2½ cm. from spine. White end papers; all edges cut.

A few copies of the first printing were bound in black leather, with semi-flexible covers; lettering in gold on backstrip similar to that on cloth copies;

front and back covers blank except for blind stamped single lines inset 3 mm. from edges. All edges cut, top edges gilt; white end papers.

Sampson Low, Marston & Co., Ltd., 1930 (February)

The Golden | Goat | By | Donn Byrne | London | Sampson Low, Marston & Co., Ltd.

Collation: 12mo (19 x 13½ cm.). 156 p. End paper; flyleaf and verso, blank; [i] half-title: The Golden Goat; [ii] Other Novels by Mr. Donn Byrne | [rule] | (list follows); [iii] title page, as above; [iv] Made and printed in Great Britain by Purnell and Sons | Paulton (Somerset) and London; 1–5, Prologue; [6] blank; 7–156, text; followed by blank flyleaf and verso, and end paper. Not illustrated. 5/.

Binding: Bound in black cloth, lettered as follows: *Backstrip:* (in gold) The | Golden | Goat | Donn | Byrne | Sampson Low   *Front cover:* (blind stamped) The Golden | Goat | Donn Byrne   The whole enclosed in a blind stamped rectangle inset 4 mm. from all edges. Single gold lines across backstrip, ½ cm. from top and lower edges. White end papers; all edges cut.

Reprinted, 1930 (March); uniform edition, 1931 (April), 5/; cheaper edition, 1931 (July), 2/6; new edition, 1935 (July, November).

First editions:
Century. "First printing" on copyright page. Cloth or leather, but only a few of the latter were published in this printing.
Sampson Low. No date or statement as to printing. 1930 reprint so states.
Periodical publication: Saturday evening post, 198:32, p. 3–5, 84ff.; 33, p. 24–25, 108ff.; 34, p. 26–27, 149ff.; February 6, 13, 20, 1926. Published under the title "A Party of baccarat." Illustrated by Arthur William Brown, many more of whose illustrations appear here than in the Century volume. Also published under title "A party of baccarat" in *Grand magazine,* London, no. 288, 289; February, March, 1929. Not illustrated.

The "Prologue" which appears in the Century Co. and Sampson Low volumes, is omitted from the *Saturday evening post* and *Grand magazine* publications.

The manuscript was sold at auction in New York November 11, 1937, and is described in the American Art Association-Anderson Galleries catalogue of that date. "Baccara" and "The new shoe" are two titles which appear, crossed out, in the manuscript, which is itself entitled "The Golden Goat." The manuscript was sold for $180 to Messrs. Retz and Storm, Inc., and was subsequently offered for sale in their catalogue no. six (1938), priced at $300.

This story, an obvious pot-boiler, was written during the summer of 1924, at Newquay in Cornwall; according to Mr. Macauley's biography (p. 170), "to recoup the *coups manqués* on the Riviera."

Reviews: New York Herald Tribune books, June 1, 1930, p. 7 (Virginia Peterson Ross); *Times literary supplement,* London, 29:162, Feb. 27, 1930; *New*

RIVERS OF DAMASCUS

York Times, IV, 8:1, June 8, 1930; *Bookman*, London, 78:463, p. 60, April, 1930; *Bookman*, New York, 71:5, p. xi, July, 1930.

RIVERS OF DAMASCUS
The Century Co., 1931 (September)

Rivers | Of Damascus | And Other Stories | By | Donn Byrne | [ornament] | [publisher's device] | The Century Co. | New York London

Collation: 12mo (19½ × 13½ cm.). 365 p. End paper; flyleaf and verso, blank; [i] half-title: Rivers of Damascus | And Other Stories; [ii] blank; [iii] title page, as above; [iv] publisher's acknowledgments | copyright statement | First Printing | Printed in U. S. A.; [v] Foreword by Dorothea Donn-Byrne.; [vi] blank; [vii] Contents; [viii] blank; [1] divisional half-title: Rivers of Damascus; [2] blank; 3–365, text; followed by three blank pages, blank flyleaf and end paper. Not illustrated. $2.00.

Binding: Bound in terra cotta cloth lettered in black as follows: *Backstrip:* Rivers | Of | Damascus | [ornament] | Donn | Byrne | The | Century | Co. *Front cover:* Rivers | Of | Damascus | [ornament] | Donn | Byrne   Double black lines across backstrip and front cover, 2½ cm. from top and lower edges; similar lines vertically on front cover, 2½ cm. from sides, all enclosing lettering. Back cover blank; light brown end papers; all edges cut.

Sampson Low, Marston & Co., Ltd., 1931 (June)

Rivers | Of Damascus | And other Stories | By | Donn Byrne | London | Sampson Low, Marston & Co., Ltd.

Collation: 12mo (19 × 13½ cm.). vii, 312 p. End paper; flyleaf and verso blank; [i] half-title: Rivers of Damascus | And other Stories; [ii] Other Works by Mr. Donn Byrne | [rule] | (list follows); [iii] title page, as above; [iv] First Impression | Made and printed in Great Britain by Purnell and Sons | Paulton (Somerset) and London; v, Foreword, by Dorothea Donn-Byrne.; [vi] blank; vii, Contents; verso [viii], blank; 1–312, text; followed by blank flyleaf and verso, and end paper. Not illustrated. 7/6.

Binding: Bound in black cloth, with lettering blind stamped on front cover, and in gold on backstrip, as follows: *Backstrip:* Rivers Of | Damascus | and | other Stories | Donn | Byrne | Sampson Low   *Front cover:* Rivers of Damascus | and other Stories | Donn Byrne   Back cover blank; single gold lines across backstrip, ½ cm. from top and lower edges; white end papers; all edges cut.

Reprinted, cheaper edition, 1932 (March), 3/6 (second impression).

Contents: Rivers of Damascus. Fosterage. The colleen rue. Sea change. Graft. And did those feet. The thing called gratitude. The sound of millstones. The bride's play. A woman in the house. A wife of no importance.

DONN BYRNE BIBLIOGRAPHY

First editions:
Century. "First printing" on copyright page.
Sampson Low. "First impression" on verso of title page.
Notes on the individual stories:
Rivers of Damascus. *McCall's magazine*, 54:1, p. 10–12, 85ff.; October, 1926. Illustrated by Walter Biggs. Story placed in Group I in the 1927 edition of the *O. Henry Memorial Award prize stories*, given two asterisks, indicating special distinction, in Mr. O'Brien's 1927 anthology of Best short stories.

Fosterage. *Collier's magazine*, 75:12, p. 7–8, 28ff.; March 21, 1925. Illustrated by George Wright. Published under the title "Pipes o' glory." Given single asterisk, indicating distinction, in Mr. O'Brien's 1925 anthology of Best short stories.

The colleen rue. *Cosmopolitan magazine*, 46:6, p. 66–70, 133ff.; May, 1919. Illustrated by G. Patrick Nelson. This story was written in December, 1918; the author received $900 for it.

Sea change. *Hearst's international*, 33:4, p. 298–300, 307ff.; April, 1918. Illustrated by Anton Otto Fischer.

Graft. *Saturday evening post*, 188:43, p. 5–7, 61ff.; April 22, 1916. Illustrated. This story was singled out for special mention in Baker's *Contemporary short story* (Heath, 1916); it is also included on the "Roll of Honor" in O'Brien's 1916 anthology.

And did those feet. *Saturday evening post*, 199:22, p. 8–10, 113ff.; November 27, 1926. Illustrated by Henry Raleigh. Given two asterisks in Mr. O'Brien's 1927 anthology of Best short stories.

In a letter written from Warren Farm House October 20, 1926, Donn Byrne says: "I write very few short stories now but one will appear some week very soon which I reckon to be the best story I have done in twelve years of writing. The title is 'And Did Those Feet' . . . and Mr. Lorimer liked it so much he gave me four thousand dollars for it, — a sure mark of appreciation."

The thing called gratitude. *Hearst's international*, 41:1, p. 41–43, 70ff.; January, 1922. Illustrated by Baron Gayne de Meyer. Written in May, 1918; brought $675. Manuscript title: A thing called gratitude.

The sound of millstones. *Saturday evening post*, 189:39, p. 24–25, 102ff; March 24, 1917. Illustrated by Henry Raleigh. Given single asterisk in Mr. O'Brien's 1917 anthology.

The bride's play. *Hearst's international*, 38:3, p. 8–10, 60ff.; September, 1920. Illustrated by Norman Price. See under Cinematizations. Single asterisk in Mr. O'Brien's 1920 anthology.

A woman in the house. *Saturday evening post*, 189:36, p. 6–8, 102ff.; March 8, 1917. Illustrated by E. F. Ward. Single asterisk in Mr. O'Brien's 1917 anthology.

A wife of no importance. *Metropolitan magazine*, 54:4, p. 6–9, 57ff.; July, 1924. Illustrated by Will Grefe. Original title was "The Inseparables."

Reviews: Bookman, London, 80:480, p. 309, Sept., 1931 (Martin Mills); *New York Times*, IV, 7:3, Sept. 27, 1931; *New York Herald Tribune books*, Sept. 6, 1931, p. 12 (J. K. Atkins); *Boston Evening Transcript*, book section,

A WOMAN OF THE SHEE—SARGASSO SEA

3:1, Sept. 5, 1931; *Times literary supplement*, London, 30:584, July 23, 1931; *Spectator*, London, 147:28, July 4, 1931 (Bonamy Dobrée).

A WOMAN OF THE SHEE
SARGASSO SEA

The Century Co., 1932 (July)

A Woman | Of The Shee | And Other Stories | By | Donn Byrne | [ornament] | [publisher's device] | The Century Co. | New York | London

Collation: 12mo (19½ × 13½ cm.). vii, 317 p. End paper; flyleaf and verso, blank; [1] half-title: A Woman of the Shee | And Other Stories; [ii] Other Works by | Donn Byrne | [ornament] | (list follows); [iii] title page, as above; [iv] publisher's acknowledgments, copyright statement. First printing | Printed in U. S. A.; [v] Reveil (poem follows) | Donn Byrne | "Smart Set," New York, 1915.; [vi] blank; vii, Contents; [viii] blank; [1] divisional half-title: A Woman of the Shee; verso [2], blank; 3–317, text; followed by three blank pages, flyleaf and verso, blank, and end paper. Not illustrated. $2.00.

Binding: Terra cotta cloth, lettered in black, as follows: *Backstrip:* A Woman | Of | The Shee | [ornament] | Donn | Byrne | The | Century | Co. *Front cover:* A Woman | Of | The Shee | [ornament] | Donn | Byrne   Double black lines across backstrip and front cover, 2½ cm. from top and lower edges; similar lines vertically on front cover, 2½ cm. from margins, and enclosing lettering. Light brown end papers; all pages cut.

Sampson Low, Marston & Co., Ltd., 1932 (February)

Sargasso Sea | And other Stories | By | Donn Byrne | London | Sampson Low, Marston & Co. Ltd.

Collation: 12mo (19 × 13¼ cm.). vii, 344 p. End paper; flyleaf and verso, blank; [i] half-title: Sargasso Sea | And other Stories; [ii] Other Works by Mr. Donn Byrne. | [rule] | (list follows); [iii] title page, as above; [iv] Made and printed in Great Britain by Purnell and Sons | Paulton (Somerset) and London; v, Reveil | (poem follows) | Donn Byrne | Smart Set | New York, 1915; [vi] blank; vii, Contents; verso [viii], blank; 1–344, text; followed by blank flyleaf and verso, and end paper. Not illustrated. 7/6.

Binding: Bound in black cloth, with lettering blind stamped on front cover, and in gold on backstrip: *Backstrip:* Sargasso | Sea | and | other Stories | Donn | Byrne| Sampson Low   *Front cover:* Sargasso Sea | and other Stories | Donn Byrne   Single gold lines across backstrip, ½ cm. from top and lower edges; back cover blank. White end papers; all edges cut.

Reprinted, cheaper edition, 1932 (November), 3/6.

Contents: A woman of the shee. "O snowy-breasted pearl." Triangle. The honorable of the earth. A brevity on page three. Mrs. Alexander Tyson. A marriage has been arranged. Sargasso Sea. An infringement of the decalogue. What became of Margot Gilholme. Beulah Land. Wife of the red-haired man.

DONN BYRNE BIBLIOGRAPHY

First editions:
Century. "First printing" on copyright page.
Sampson Low. No date, no statement as to printing.
Notes on the individual stories:
A woman of the shee. *Saturday evening post,* 191:1, p. 54, 57ff.; July 6, 1918. Illustrated by E. F. Ward. Given one asterisk by Mr. O'Brien in his 1918 anthology.
"O snowy-breasted pearl." *Coloroto magazine, Chicago Tribune,* June 3, 1923, p. 10–13. Illustrated by Garrett Price.
Triangle. *Everybody's magazine,* 47:3, p. 85–95; Sept., 1922. Not illustrated.
The honorable of the earth. *Saturday evening post,* 188:30, p. 16–18, 61ff.; January 22, 1916. Illustrated by M. Leone Bracker. On Mr. O'Brien's Roll of Honor (1916).
A brevity on page three. *American magazine,* 86:4, p. 22–25, 79ff.; October, 1918. Illustrated by Paul Julien Meylan. Published under title "A case of blackmail." Written in February, 1918, and brought $360.
Mrs. Alexander Tyson. *Pictorial review,* 26:4, p. 14–16, 36ff.; January, 1925. Illustrated by Nat Little. Published under title "Green Eyes." Listed in Group II in the 1925 volume of *O. Henry Memorial Award prize stories,* given one asterisk in Mr. O'Brien's anthology of the same year.
A marriage has been arranged. *Hearst's international,* 39:5, p. 10–12, 83ff.; May, 1921. Illustrated by Walter Everett.
Sargasso Sea. *Saturday evening post,* 189:11, p. 3–5, 41ff.; September 9, 1916. Illustrated by F. R. Gruger. On Mr. O'Brien's 1916 Roll of Honor.
An infringement of the decalogue. *Hearst's international,* 32:6, p. 473–475, 500ff.; December, 1917. Illustrated by M. Leone Bracker.
What became of Margot Gilholme. *Hearst's international,* 39:1, p. 11–13, 58; January, 1921. Illustrated by Will Foster. Contents page of same issue bears photograph of Donn Byrne. The typescript of this story is marked "No. 121;" it bears the original title "People of unimportance;" is signed at Riverside, Conn.
Beulah Land. *Cosmopolitan magazine,* 46:5, p. 67–71, 90ff.; April, 1919. Illustrated by M. Leone Bracker. Written in November, 1918, brought $900. One asterisk in Mr. O'Brien's 1919 volume.
The wife of the red-haired man. *Red book,* 31:2, p. 23–29, 135ff.; June, 1918. Illustrated by M. Leone Bracker. One asterisk in Mr. O'Brien's 1918 anthology.
Reviews: Boston Evening Transcript, July 16, 1932, p. 2 (Karl Schriftgiesser); *New York Herald Tribune books,* July 24, 1932, p. 6; *New York Times,* v, 14:2, July 24, 1932; *Times literary supplement,* London, 31:204, March 17, 1932; *Spectator,* London, 148:264, Feb. 20, 1932 (L. A. G. Strong).
Miss Fanny Butcher writes in the *Chicago Tribune* of July 26, 1932, about Donn Byrne and about the comments she received regarding her review of WoS the previous week. Presumably the date of this review was July 19th.

THE ISLAND OF YOUTH
The Appleton-Century Co., 1933 (August)

The | Island Of Youth | And Other Stories | By | Donn Byrne | The Century Co. | New York   London

Collation: 12mo (19 x 13½ cm.). v, 282 p. End paper; flyleaf and verso, blank; [i] half-title: The Island Of Youth | And Other Stories; [ii] Other Works by

THE ISLAND OF YOUTH

Donn Byrne | [rule] | (list follows); [iii] title page, as above; [iv] Made and printed in Great Britain by Purnell and Sons | Paulton (Somerset) and London; v, Contents, verso [vi], blank; 1–282, text, followed by flyleaf and verso, blank, and end paper. Not illustrated. $1.75.

Binding: Bound in terra cotta cloth, with lettering in black, as follows: *Backstrip:* The | Island | Of Youth | [ornament] | Donn | Byrne | Appleton | Century *Front cover:* The | Island | Of Youth | [ornament] | Donn | Byrne   Back cover blank. Double black lines extending across backstrip and front cover 2 cm. from top and lower edges, similar lines vertically on front cover 2½cm. from sides, enclosing lettering. Light brown end papers and flyleaf; all edges cut.

Note: Publisher's name is "The Century Co." on title page; "Appleton-Century" on backstrip.

Sampson Low, Marston & Co., Ltd., 1932 (October)

The | Island Of Youth | And Other Stories | By | Donn Byrne | London | Sampson Low, Marston & Co., Ltd.

Collation: 12mo (19 x 13½ cm.). v, 282 p. End paper; flyleaf and verso, blank; [i] half-title: The Island Of Youth | And Other Stories; [ii] Other Works by Mr. Donn Byrne | [rule] | (list follows); [iii] title page, as above; [iv] Made and printed in Great Britain by Purnell and Sons | Paulton (Somerset) and London; v, Contents; verso [vi], blank; 1–282, text; followed by blank flyleaf and verso, and end paper. Not illustrated. 7/6.

Binding: Bound in black cloth, with lettering in gold on backstrip, and blind stamped on front cover: *Backstrip:* The | Island | Of | Youth | Donn | Byrne | Sampson Low   *Front cover:* The | Island Of Youth | Donn Byrne   Single gold lines across backstrip, ½ cm. from top and lower edges. Back cover blank. White end papers; all edges cut.

Reprinted, uniform edition, 1933; cheaper edition, 1933 (July), 3/6.

Texts of Appleton-Century and Sampson Low editions appear to be printed from same plates.

Contents: The island of youth. The great gift. The gryphon. The lion in the streets. Superdirigible "Gamma-1." The portrait of Marian Long. The parable of the Bad Samaritan. The miracle of Bethesda. A manner of legacy.

First editions:
Appleton-Century. No date; no statement as to printing.
Sampson Low. No date; no statement as to printing.

Notes on the individual stories:
The island of youth. *Ladies' home journal,* 33:11, p. 11, 103ff.; 12, p. 15, 83ff.; 34:1, p. 14, 49ff.; November, December, 1916; January, 1917. Illustrated by Arthur E. Becher.

The great gift. *Hearst's international,* 39:7, p. 13–15, 62ff.; July, 1921. Illustrated by Walter Everett. Original title of this story was "Telepathy." (See *Hearst's international,* May, 1921, p. 82.) This story was given one asterisk in Mr. O'Brien's 1921 Roll of Honor.

The gryphon. *Saturday evening post*, 189:44, p. 16–18, 37ff.; April 28, 1917. Illustrated by E. F. Ward. Miss Williams' *Handbook on story writing* (Dodd, Mead, 1918) makes specific mention of this story as an example of short story technique.

The lion in the streets. *American Sunday monthly magazine*, p. 4–6; July 2, 1916. Illustrated by W. A. Hottinger.

Superdingible "Gamma-1." *Scribner's magazine*, 60:2, p. 160–170; August, 1916. Illustrated by F. C. Yohn. (See also, *ibid*., p. 8, for publisher's announcement, and mention of "Underseaboat F-33.")

Mr. Jessup's *Representative short stories* (New York, 1923) refers specifically to this story as well as to "Biplane No. 2." Mr. Baker's *Contemporary short story* (New York, 1916) also singles out this story for particular mention. Included in Mr. O'Brien's 1916 "Roll of Honor."

The portrait of Marian Long. *Hearst's international*, 32:3, p. 186–187, 220ff.; September, 1917. Illustrated by W. T. Benda.

The parable of the Bad Samaritan. *American Sunday monthly magazine*, September 3, 1916, p. 5–7, 16ff. Illustrated by James Montgomery Flagg.

The miracle of Bethesda. *Hearst's international*, 35:2, p. 11–13, 58ff.; February, 1919. Illustrated by F. Walter Taylor. Written in June, 1918, sold for $810.

A manner of legacy. *Metropolitan magazine*, 59:6, p. 16–20, 71ff.; September, 1924. Illustrated by Delos Palmer. Published under title "The Sister act." Original title, "Bart Treddick's daughter" (see *Hearst's international*, January, 1922, p. 66)

Reviews: *New York Herald Tribune books*, Aug. 27, 1933, p. 11 (Norah Meade); *New York Times*, v, 7:4, Aug. 13, 1933; *Boston Evening Transcript*, Sept. 6, 1933, p. 2; *New York Sun*, Aug. 19, 1933 (Kathleen R. E. Hood); *Times literary supplement*, London, 31:791, Oct. 27, 1932.

AN ALLEY OF FLASHING SPEARS

Appleton-Century Co., 1934 (July)

An Alley Of | Flashing Spears | And Other Stories | By | Donn Byrne | [publisher's device] | D. Appleton-Century Company | Incorporated | New York 1934

Collation: 12mo (19 × 13 cm.). v, 250 p. End paper; flyleaf and verso, blank; [i] half-title: An Alley Of Flashing Spears | And Other Stories; [ii] blank; [iii] title page, as above; verso [iv], Made and printed in Great Britain; v, Contents; verso [vi], blank; [1] divisional half-title: An Alley Of Flashing Spears | And Other Stories; verso [2], blank; 3–250, text; followed by blank flyleaf and verso, and end paper. Not illustrated. $2.00.

Binding: Bound in terra cotta cloth, lettered in black as follows: *Backstrip:* An Alley | Of Flashing | Spears | [ornament] | Donn | Byrne | Appleton | Century *Front cover:* An Alley | Of Flashing | Spears | [ornament] | Donn | Byrne Back cover blank. Double black lines across backstrip and front cover, 2½ cm. from top and lower edges; similar lines vertically on front cover, 2 cm. from sides and enclosing lettering. White end papers; all edges cut.

AN ALLEY OF FLASHING SPEARS

Sampson Low, Marston & Co., Ltd., 1933 (February)

An Alley Of | Flashing Spears | And Other Stories | By | Donn Byrne | London | Sampson Low, Marston & Co., Ltd.

Collation: 12mo (19 x 13 cm.). v, 250 p. End paper; flyleaf and verso, blank; [i] half-title: An Alley Of Flashing Spears | And Other Stories; [ii] Other Works by Mr. Donn Byrne | [rule] | (list follows); [iii] title page, as above; [iv] Made and printed in Great Britain by Purnell and Sons | Paulton (Somerset) and London; v, Contents; [vi] blank; [1] divisional half-title: An Alley of Flashing Spears | And Other Stories; verso [2], blank; 3–250, text; followed by blank flyleaf and verso, and end paper. Not illustrated. 7/6.

Binding: Bound in black cloth, with lettering in gold on backstrip and blind stamped on front cover, as follows: *Backstrip:* An Alley | Of | Flashing | Spears | Donn | Byrne | Sampson Low   *Front cover:* An Alley Of | Flashing Spears | Donn Byrne   Back cover blank; narrow gold lines across backstrip, ½ cm. from top and lower edges; white end papers; all edges cut.

Reprinted, cheaper edition, 1933 (December), 3/6; new edition, 1934 (May).

Texts of Appleton-Century and Sampson Low editions appear to be printed from same plates.

Contents: An alley of flashing spears. Treachery. The master of Raymond Lully. Executive session. Towers of silence. The happy townland. Hail and farewell. Green isle. A sister of shining swords.

First editions:

Appleton-Century. Date on title page; no statement as to printing.

Sampson Low. No date or statement as to printing.

Notes on the individual stories:

An alley of flashing spears. *Saturday evening post,* 189:17, p. 10–13, 33ff.; October 21, 1916. Illustrated by M. Leone Bracker. Mr. Byrne sold the motion picture rights to this story to the New York Motion Picture Corporation (Triangle Kay-Bee Photoplays), for $500.00, one week after its appearance in the *Post.* Mr. O'Brien's 1916 anthology lists this story on the Roll of Honor, without further comment.

Treachery. *Hearst's international,* 42:2, p. 49–51, 117ff.; August, 1922. Illustrated by Baron de Meyer. Magazine title: "Paul and Ruth and Solomon."

The master of Raymond Lully. *American Sunday monthly magazine,* June 4, 1916; p. 10–13. Illustrated by William Hottinger.

Executive session. *Hearst's international,* 31:1, p. 24–25, 58; January, 1917. Illustrated by M. Leone Bracker.

Towers of silence. *Hearst's international,* 36:4, p. 29–31, 88; October, 1919. Illustrated by Walter H. Everett.

Hail and farewell. Magazine and date of publication not known.

The happy townland. *Red book,* 30:2, p. 49–54, 133f.; December, 1917. Illustrated by Oscar Frederick Howard. Accompanying "blurb" mentions two other Donn Byrne stories which appeared in this magazine, "The crown of Sheba's Queen" and "A quatrain of Ling Tai Fu's."

Green Isle. *Hearst's international,* 36:1, p. 11–13, 72ff.; July, 1919. Illustrated by Anton Otto Fischer.

A sister of shining swords. *Collier's magazine*, 61·11, p. 12–13, 26ff.; May 25, 1918. Illustrated by J. Scott Williams. This story was written in March, 1918, probably at Larchmont, and brought the author $450.00. Given single asterisk in Mr. O'Brien's 1918 anthology.

Reviews: Boston Evening Transcript, July 25, 1934, p. 3; *Chicago News*, Aug. 8, 1934 (T. J. Tiernan); *New York Times*, v, 7:5, July 29, 1934 (Margaret Wallace); *New York World-Telegram*, Aug. 16, 1934 (Pierre Loving); *Times literary supplement*, London, 32:148, March 2, 1933.

THE HOUND OF IRELAND

Appleton-Century Co., 1935 (January 16)

The | Hound Of Ireland | And Other Stories | By | Donn Byrne | [publisher's device] | D. Appleton-Century Company | Incorporated | New York 1935.

Collation: 12mo (19 x 13½ cm.). v, 250 p. End paper; flyleaf and verso, blank; [i] half-title: The Hound Of Ireland | And Other Stories; verso [ii], blank; [iii] title page, as above; verso [iv], Made and printed in Great Britain; v, Contents; verso [vi], blank; 1–250, text; followed by blank flyleaf and end paper. Not illustrated. $2.00.

Binding: Bound in terra cotta cloth lettered in black as follows: *Backstrip:* The Hound | Of | Ireland | [ornament] | Donn | Byrne | Appleton | Century   *Front:* The Hound | Of | Ireland | [ornament] | Donn | Byrne   Back cover blank; across backstrip and front cover, double black lines 2½ cm. from top and lower edges; similar lines on front cover, perpendicular, 2 cm from sides, enclosing the lettering. White end papers. All edges cut.

Sampson Low, Marston & Co., Ltd., 1934 (January)

The | Hound Of Ireland | And other Stories | By | Donn Byrne | London | Sampson Low, Marston & Co., Ltd.

Collation: 12mo (19 x 13½ cm.). v, 250 p. End paper; flyleaf and verso, blank; [i] half-title: The Hound Of Ireland | And other Stories; [ii] Other works by Mr. Donn Byrne | [rule] | (list follows); [iii] title page, as above; verso [iv], Made and printed in Great Britain by Purnell and Sons | Paulton (Somerset) and London; v, Contents; verso [vi], blank; 1–250; text; followed by blank flyleaf and verso, and end paper. No illustrations. 7/6.

Binding: Bound in black cloth, with lettering blind stamped on front cover and in gold on backstrip, as follows: *Backstrip:* The | Hound Of | Ireland | Donn | Byrne | Sampson Low   *Front cover:* The Hound | Of Ireland | Donn Byrne   Back cover blank; single gold lines across backstrip, ½ cm. from top and lower edges; white end papers; all edges cut.

Reprinted, cheaper edition, 1934 (November), 3/6.

Contents: The hound of Ireland. Fiddler's Green. Mrs. Dutton intervenes. Underseaboat F–33. Sentiment. The day after to-morrow. Bargain price. The bronze box.

A DAUGHTER OF THE MEDICI

First editions·
Appleton-Century. Date on title page; no statement as to printing.
Sampson Low. No date or statement as to printing.
Text of American and English editions appears to be printed from same plates.
Notes on the individual stories·
The hound of Ireland. *Collier's magazine,* 71:5, p. 3–4, 24ff.; February 3, 1923. Illustrated by G. Patrick Nelson. See *ibid* , p. 30, for portrait. Given single asterisk in Mr. O'Brien's 1923 anthology, and inclusion on "Roll of Honor" in the 1927 volume.

Fiddler's Green. *Saturday evening post,* 190:34, p. 9–11, 34ff.; February 23, 1918. Illustrated by E. F. Ward. Given single asterisk in Mr. O'Brien's 1918 volume.

Mrs. Dutton intervenes. *American Sunday monthly magazine,* May 7, 1916; p. 6–7, 18f. Illustrated by T. D. Skidmore. Given single asterisk by Mr. O'Brien in 1916 anthology.

Underseaboat F–33. *Scribner's magazine,* 59:5, p. 28–38; January, 1916. Illustrated by W. J. Aylward. See note on "Superdirigible 'Gamma–1'." Given triple asterisk in Mr. O'Brien's 1916 anthology, and two asterisks in that of 1920.

Sentiment. *Snappy stories,* 14:1, p. 29–36; October, 1915. Not illustrated.

The day after to-morrow. *McClure's magazine,* 49:6, p. 18–19, 50ff.; October, 1917. Illustrated by Thomas Fogarty. Typescript of this story is marked "No. 47"; the script is dated Nov. 7, 1916, and bears two preliminary titles, "Civic pride" and "The people of the State of New York." Mr. O'Brien gives this story two asterisks in his 1917 anthology.

Bargain price. *Cosmopolitan magazine,* 46:4, p. 53–57, 135ff.; March, 1919. Illustrated by John Alonzo Williams. Written in October, 1918, and sold for $810.00.

Despite Mr. Macauley's statement that the story appeared in the O. Henry Memorial Award volume for 1919 (*Donn Byrne, bard of Armagh,* p. 214), this was not actually the case, although it is mentioned in this book (p. ix), and is listed in "Group I." Mr. Macauley possibly obtained this misinformation from the *Bookman* of April, 1920 (51:2, p. 253) where the same statement is made. Story is not listed in Mr. O'Brien's 1919 volume.

The bronze box. *Ladies' home journal,* 33:1, p. 11–12; 2, p. 25–26; 3, p. 28, 95, 97; January – March, 1916. Illustrated by Charles E. Chambers.

Reviews: New York Times, v, 16:5, Feb. 10, 1935; *New York Herald Tribune books,* Feb. 3, 1935, p. 8 (Geoffrey Terwilliger); *Times literary supplement,* London, 33:110, Feb. 15, 1934; *New York Sun,* Feb. 2, 1935 (Arthur Heinemann).

A DAUGHTER OF THE MEDICI
Appleton-Century Co., 1935 (July 8)

A Daughter Of | The Medici | And Other Stories | By | Donn Byrne | [publisher's device] | D. Appleton-Century Company | Incorporated | New York 1935

Collation: 12mo (19 x 13½ cm.). v, 282 p. End paper; flyleaf and verso, blank; [i] half-title: A Daughter Of The Medici | And Other Stories; verso [ii], blank;

[iii] title page, as above; [iv] Made and printed in Great Britain; v, Contents; verso [vi], blank; 1–282, text; followed by blank flyleaf and verso, and end paper. Not illustrated. $2.00.

Binding: Bound in terra cotta cloth lettered in black as follows: *Backstrip:* A Daughter | Of The | Medici | [ornament] | Donn | Byrne | Appleton | Century *Front cover.* A Daughter | Of The | Medici | [ornament] | Donn | Byrne Double black lines 2½ cm. from top and lower edges across backstrip and front cover; similar lines on front cover extending vertically 2 cm. from edges. Ornaments at the four corners, outside the rectangle. Back cover blank; white end papers; all edges cut.

Sampson Low, Marston & Co., Ltd., 1933 (September)

A Daughter Of | The Medici | And Other Stories | By | Donn Byrne | London | Sampson Low, Marston & Co., Ltd.

Collation: 12mo (19 × 13½ cm.). v, 282 p. End paper; flyleaf and verso, blank; [i] half-title: A Daughter Of The Medici | And Other Stories; [ii], Other works by Mr. Donn Byrne | [rule] | (list follows); [iii] title page, as above; verso [iv], Made and printed in Great Britain by Purnell and Sons | Paulton (Somerset) and London; v, Contents; verso [vi], blank; 1–282, text; followed by flyleaf and verso, blank, and end paper. Not illustrated. 7/6.

Binding: Bound in black cloth with lettering blind stamped on front cover, and in gold on backstrip, as follows: *Backstrip:* A | Daughter | Of The | Medici | Donn | Byrne | Sampson Low   *Front cover:* A Daughter Of | The Medici | Donn Byrne Back cover blank; white end papers; all edges cut.

Reprinted, cheaper edition, 1934 (August, December), 3/6; new edition, 1935 (January).

Contents: A daughter of the Medici. Champions. A happy ending. A certain regrettable occasion. Anti-climax. The cock-and-bull story of Captain Patrick Burgoyne. The evil men do. As to impediments. Harley Johnston, gentleman.

First editions:

Appleton-Century. Date on title page. No statement as to printing.

Sampson Low. No date or statement as to printing.

Texts of American and English editions appear to be printed from same plates.

Notes on the individual stories:

A daughter of the Medici. *Hearst's international*, 40:3, p. 6–8, 72ff., September, 1921. Illustrated by Will Foster. Included in Mr. O'Brien's 1921 listing, but not awarded any special distinction.

Champions. *Blue book*, 25:2, p. 225–234; June, 1917. Illustrated by Herbert Morton Stoops. At the time of this publication, Ray Long was editor of the *Blue book*; his comment on this story, as given on the contents page, "The best story of a prize-fight we have ever printed."

A happy ending. *Hearst's international*, 41:4, p. 11–13, 91ff.; April, 1922. Illustrated by Charles D. Mitchell. Also included without comment in Mr. O'Brien's annual (1922) listing.

POEMS

A certain regrettable occasion. *Harper's bazaar,* 60.7, p. 90–91, 117ff.; July, 1925. Illustrated by John La Gatta. Given single asterisk in Mr. O'Brien's 1925 anthology.

Anti-climax. *Hearst's international,* 35:6, p. 11–13, 74ff.; June, 1919. Illustrated by Lejaren à Hiller. This story was written in June, 1918, and sold for $675.00.

The cock-and-bull story of Captain Patrick Burgoyne. *American Sunday monthly magazine,* August 6, 1916; p. 3–4, 17ff. Illustrated by William Hottinger. Given single asterisk in Mr. O'Brien's 1916 anthology.

The evil men do. *Metropolitan magazine,* 59:5, p. 14–17, 79ff.; August, 1924. Illustrated by G. Patrick Nelson. The original title of this story was "The rumbling drum"; later this was changed to "A Rubai of El Khayyam's"; the typescript shows the former lined out and the latter substituted. The typescript is of further interest in that it bears many changes, corrections, etc., in the author's handwriting, unlike most of the others. Story is listed, without comment, in Mr. O'Brien's 1924 annual.

As to impediments. *Hearst's international,* 44.1, p. 49–51, 107ff.; July, 1923. Illustrated by Everett Shinn. "The captain's bride." Story was originally announced in *Hearst's international* for September, 1920 (38:3, p. 60), but was not actually published until almost three years later. Given one asterisk by Mr. O'Brien in 1923.

Harley Johnston, gentleman. *Snappy stories,* 11:1, p. 1–23; February, 1915. Not illustrated. This story is of some interest in that it is characteristic of the writer's early work for the pulp magazines, before he had developed a market in more pretentious journals.

Reviews: *New York Times,* VI, 18:3, July 21, 1935; *New York Herald Tribune books,* July 21, 1935, p. 10; *Saturday review of literature,* 12:21, Aug. 10, 1935 (D. P.); *Times literary supplement,* London, 32:652, Sept. 28, 1933; *New York Sun,* July 20, 1935; *New York World-Telegram,* July 12, 1935 (Harry Hansen).

POEMS

Sampson Low, Marston & Co., Ltd., 1934 (May)

Poems | By | Donn Byrne | Introduction | By | Dorothea Donn-Byrne | London | Sampson Low, Marston & Co., Ltd. | MCMXXXIV

Collation: 8vo (23 × 15 cm.). viii, 44 p. End paper; flyleaf and verso, blank; [i] half-title: Poems; verso [ii], blank; [iii] title page, as above; verso [iv], Made and printed in Great Britain | by Purnell and Sons | Paulton (Somerset) and London; v, Introduction, continued to vi; vii–viii, Contents; [1] divisional half-title: Early Poems; verso [2], blank; 3–44, text; followed by flyleaf and verso, blank, and end paper. Not illustrated. 5/.

Binding: Bound in blue-green cloth, lettered in gold as follows: *Backstrip* (vertically): Poems by Donn Byrne *Front cover:* Poems | Donn Byrne White end papers; rag paper; uncut.

Contents: Early poems: The piper. The country of the young. Réveil. The King of Ireland's daughter. The kingdom of Thule. Nocturne. A ballade of old-time captains. The poet reproves etc. For a guitar. The dotage of Duns Scotus. Lines from "O snowy-breasted pearl." Beannacht Leat. *Later poems* Lines from "Blind Raftery." Lines from "Ireland, the rock whence I was hewn." *Six poems from the Gaelic:* Introduction. The girl with the grand fair head. The shallow world. The red-haired man's wife Open the door, Peter. The Roman earl. The coolin.

First edition. Date on title page, not subsequently reprinted.

Miss Davids' biographical notes, elsewhere referred to in this volume, contain the following statement regarding Mr. Byrne as a poet: "Mr. Donn Byrne was first known for his poetry. The first thing published in an American magazine was a poem, 'The Piper,' in Harper's. He turned to prose because he did not believe in the rhyming of consonants. He believed rhythm to be more important than metre . . ."

Notes on the individual poems.

The piper. *Harper's magazine*, 124:741, p. 461, February, 1912. Reprinted *Literary digest*, 44.349, February 17, 1912, *Current literature*, 53:5, p. 596, November, 1912; Thurston Macauley, *Donn Byrne, bard of Armagh; Bookman*, New York, 69:2, p. 157, April, 1929; A. E. Malone, *Donn Byrne, an Irish realist.* See also in Anthology List. Manuscript of this poem is in the Library of Congress; it bears the title "The piper hears the summer pleading."

The country of the young. *Smart set*, 42.4, p. 88; April, 1914. Reprinted *Literary digest*, 48:707, March 28, 1914. Poem is mentioned in the *Bulletin* of the Poetry Society of America, April, 1914. See Gen. Ref. List, no. 336 (1914).

Réveil. *Smart set*, 47:2, p. 124; October, 1915. Reprinted in Century Co. and Sampson Low editions of *A woman of the shee* and in several reviews of the above, as that of the *Boston Transcript*, July 16, 1932. See also Anthology List. See Gen. Ref. List, no. 336 (1916).

The king of Ireland's daughter. No prior publication of this poem has been located up to the present time, but it is believed to have appeared in print previous to its appearance in this volume.

The kingdom of Thule. *Smart set*, 47:4, p. 142; December, 1915. For reprints see Anthology List. The poem is mentioned in the November, 1915, issue of the *Bulletin* of the Poetry Society of America. Manuscript is in the Library of Congress; it bears the title "Nighttime in Lyonesse." Several textual variations are present. See Gen. Ref. List, no. 336 (1916).

Nocturne. *Smart set*, 43:4, p. 76; August, 1914. In its magazine appearance, the poem is credited to "Byron Dunne." This is one of the very few instances in which the author wrote under a pseudonym; the reason in this instance was that the same issue of the magazine contained his short story "Donoghu's hour," and it was contrary to the policy of the editors to have an author represented by more than one contribution in any single issue. See Gen. Ref. List, no. 336 (1914).

A ballade of old-time captains. *Smart set*, 42:3, p. 64; March, 1914. Reprinted *Literary digest*, 48:450, February 28, 1914. See also, *Bookman*, New York, 54:5 (January, 1922), letter from Maxwell Aley to John Farrar. Received mention in Poetry Society *Bulletin* of March, 1914. See Gen. Ref. List, no. 336 (1914).

The poet reproves certain philosophers who would lead him to wisdom. No previous publication of this poem has been found, but as in the case of "The king of Ireland's daughter" it probably did appear, possibly in one of the "little" magazines.

POEMS

For a guitar. *Smart set*, 44:1, p. 130; September, 1914. Manuscript is in the Library of Congress. It bears the title "Of Paracelsus: how love constrained him," and contains several stanzas not included in the magazine or book versions. See Gen. Ref. List, no. 336 (1914).

The dotage of Duns Scotus. *Smart set*, 41:2, p. 96; October, 1913. Reprinted *Current opinion*, 55.438; December, 1913 (with comment to the effect that this poem was one of the five best, by members of the Poetry Society, appearing in the October magazines, and that it was read at the October meeting of the Society). Manuscript is in the Library of Congress. Gen. Ref. List, no. 336 (1913).

Beannacht Leat. *Smart set*, 42.1, p. 142; January, 1914. Reprinted *Literary digest*, 48:32; January 3, 1914 (with critical comment). Poetry Society *Bulletin* (January, 1914) mentions it. See Gen. Ref. List, no. 336 (1914).

Lines from "Blind Raftery." First publication was in the magazine appearance of this story. Most of the manuscript of this verse is in the Wetherbee Collection; in addition to a number of manuscript pages there are rough notes on many of the poems, scribbled on the backs of old envelopes, etc., together with golf scores and other irrelevant material. Much if not all of this seems to have been written at Warren Farm House, Guildford, in the summer of 1923.

Lines from "Ireland, the rock whence I was hewn." First published in the *National geographic magazine*, March, 1927.

Six poems from the Gaelic. *Bookman*, New York, 55:4, p. 351–353; June, 1922. "Five poems from the Gaelic" (omits "The coolin" as a separate poem, and includes these verses as part of "The girl with the grand fair head").

Reviews: *Times literary supplement*, London, 33:427, June 14, 1934; *Bookman*, London, 86:513, p. 177, June, 1934.

The Short Stories

SHORT STORIES NOT REPRINTED IN BOOK FORM

All three in one noose. *Hearst's international*, 37:5, p. 14–15, 64f.; June, 1920. Illustrated by James H. Crank. Original title (on typescript) "One noose."

Ambition Alley. *Pictorial review*, 24:2, p. 22–23, 76ff.; November, 1922 Illustrated by Harley Ennis Stivers. The typescript is annotated in Donn Byrne's hand, "No. 63. 5500 words." Mr. O'Brien gives this story an asterisk, indicative of distinction, in his 1922 anthology of *Best short stories*.

The balance of might. *McBride's magazine*, 96:574, p. 35–44; October, 1915. Not illustrated. Editor's "blurb," *ibid.*, p. 160 Mr. Macauley makes special mention of this story in his biography (p. 48), as does Mr. Greenberg in his thesis (p. 31); Mr. O'Brien gives it a single asterisk in the 1915 anthology.

Battle. *Smart set*, 42:2, p. 103–104, February, 1914. Not illustrated. Frequently referred to as the first published story by Donn Byrne. See Macauley (p. 36–37); articles by McCardell, Malone, Kunitz, et al. (in Gen. Ref. List). The author himself authenticates this in his brief sketch in the Schnittkind and Baker *Best college stories* volume. (See under "Miscellaneous Writings.")

Clay feet. *Collier's magazine*, 61:17, p. 8–9, 26ff.; July 6, 1918. Illustrated by James Montgomery Flagg. This story was written in April, 1918, probably at Larchmont; it brought the author $450.00.

Confiteor. *Snappy stories*, 10:3, p. 65–70; January, 1915. Not illustrated.

The crown of Sheba's queen. *Red book*, 29:5, p. 849–862, 1037–1040; 29:6, p. 77–82, 150–156; September, October, 1917. Illustrated by Richard Culter.

Devised and bequeathed. *Popular magazine*, 36:5, p. 134–172; 36.6, p. 166–195; May 23, June 7, 1915. Not illustrated.

The Epistle to the Ephesians *Popular magazine*, 41:1, p. 54–61; June 20, 1916. Not illustrated.

Eve and the gopher. *McBride's magazine*, 96:576, p. 145–151; December, 1915. Not illustrated.

Fantee. *American Sunday monthly magazine*, p. 5–6, 16f.; December 5, 1915. Illustrated by T. D. Skidmore.

Her last chance. *Metropolitan magazine*, 58.2, p 22–25, 98ff.; November, 1923. Illustrated by A. Palumbo.

His Honor the Court. *Hearst's magazine*, 33:5, p. 356–357, 396f.; May, 1918. Illustrated by Walter Tittle.

London nights (a series). I. The night of Colonel Cray, Retired. *Snappy stories*, 11:2, p. 31–38; March, 1915. II. The night of the dancer in red. *ibid.*, 11:3, p. 43–48; April, 1915. III. The night of the profligate poet. *ibid.*, 12:1, p. 35–41; May, 1915. IV. The night of the singing priest. *ibid.*, 12:2, p. 81–87; June, 1915. V. The night of O'Donnell Pasha. *ibid.*, 12:3, p. 43–49; July, 1915. VI. The night of the Black Mass. *ibid.*, 13:1, p. 41–47; August, 1915.

The meditations of Kerry Macfarlane. See under "Destiny Bay."

One woman. *Snappy stories*, 10:1, p. 53–58; November, 1914. Not illustrated.

Patrick Leary's son. *Everybody's magazine*, 39:2, p. 51–56, 99–101; August, 1918. Illustrated by Charles Sarka. Written in April, 1918, probably at Larch-

THE SHORT STORIES

mont; sold for $450.00. Mr. O'Brien gives this story a single asterisk, indicating distinction, in his 1918 anthology.

The prodigal in Utopia. *Saturday evening post,* 190:10, p. 20–22, 109ff.; September 8, 1917. Illustrated by Henry Raleigh. Also given one asterisk by Mr. O'Brien in his 1917 volume.

The purling brook which is Bow Sing Low's. *Popular magazine,* 49:2, p. 158–166; July 7, 1918. Not illustrated. Written in March, 1918, and sold for $270.00.

The ruby rose. *McBride's magazine,* 97:579, p. 41–52; March, 1916. Not illustrated.

Sinister hand. *American short story magazine,* February, 1930; p. 5–17. Not illustrated. Given single asterisk in Mr. O'Brien's 1930 anthology.

Sorrentina. *See under* "Miscellaneous Writings."

Steering-gear. *Snappy stories,* 13:2, p. 21–27; September, 1915. Not illustrated. Donn Byrne's copy of this issue of *Snappy stories* bears the notes, "No. 33. 4,124 words."

The supreme sacrifice. *Macfadden fiction lovers' magazine,* 40:1, p. 49–52, 90ff.; October, 1924. Illustrated by Delos Palmer. Given a single asterisk in Mr. O'Brien's 1925 anthology.

Hearst's international for July, 1921, announces a story soon to appear in that magazine; although the title is given as "Lazara," the name of the heroine is stated to be "Janet Maxwell"; the latter is the chief character of "The supreme sacrifice." Similarly, "A bill of divorcement" was announced for publication in *Hearst's* to appear late in 1921 or early in 1922. As neither "Lazara" nor "A bill of divorcement" ever did appear in *Hearst's,* it is apparent that this story was turned over to the Macfadden magazine, and published there with still another title. This hypothesis is confirmed by personal communications from the publishers and from Mrs. Donn-Byrne.

Sweet honey in all mouths. *Saturday evening post,* 190:41, p. 14–15, 105ff.; April 13, 1918. Illustrated by E. F. Ward. Written in January, 1918; sold for $450. Listed in Mr. O'Brien's 1918 anthology of *Best short stories,* but not accorded any special distinction.

Through "Hell" to peace. *Smart set,* 44:1, p. 97–111; September, 1914. Not illustrated. In connection with this story, the following excerpt from a letter written by a former friend and colleague of Donn Byrne's is of some interest: "I remember very well his excitement over the fact that the editors of the 'Smart Set', H. L. Mencken and George Jean Nathan, had changed the cover of the magazine for the first time in its history in honor of his story 'Through "Hell" to Peace'; certainly the first and, I think, one of the best of the German invasion of America stories." The cover in question depicts a battle scene over which the title of the story is superimposed; beneath is the legend: "A great sensational story of the present war. How American brains vanquished chaos and compelled peace."

A treasure upon earth. *Saturday evening post,* 190:18, p. 5–8, 44ff.; November 3, 1917. Illustrated by R. F. James. Given single asterisk by Mr. O'Brien in his 1917 volume. This story was written at Port Jefferson, N. Y.; the author's contract with the *Saturday evening post* is dated September 4, 1917, and calls for a $250 advance payment against a total price of $1750.

DONN BYRNE BIBLIOGRAPHY

ALPHABETICAL LIST OF SHORT STORIES

Abbreviations

AoFS	Alley of Flashing Spears
Ch	Changeling
DB	Destiny Bay
DoM	Daughter of the Medici
HH	Hangman's House
HoI	Hound of Ireland
IoY	Island of Youth
RoD	Rivers of Damascus
SwW	Stories without Women
WB	Wind Bloweth
WoS	Woman of the Shee

An Alphabetical List

An African epic (SwW)
All three in one noose
An Alley of flashing spears (AoFS)
Ambition Alley
And did those feet — (RoD)
And Zabad begat Ephlal (see Belfasters)
Anti-climax (DoM)
The Arab lady (see Wisdom buildeth her house)
As to impediments (DoM)
The Balance of might
Bargain price (HoI)
The Barnacle goose (Ch)
Bart Treddick's daughter (see A Manner of legacy)
Battle
Belfasters (Ch)
Beulah Land (WoS)
A Bill of divorcement (see The Supreme sacrifice)
Biplane No. 2 (SwW)
Black magic (see Black Medicine)
Black medicine (SwW)
Blackmail (see A Brevity on page three)

Blue waves of Tory (HH)
Bow Sing Low and the two who were thieves (SwW)
A Brevity on page three (WoS)
The Bride's play (RoD)
The Bronze box (HoI)
By ordeal of justice (Ch)
The Captain's bride (see As to impediments)
A Case of blackmail (see A Brevity on page three)
A Certain regrettable occasion (DoM)
Champions (DoM)
Changeling (Ch)
Civic pride (see The Day after tomorrow)
Clay feet
The Cock-and-bull story of Captain Burgoyne (DoM)
The Colleen rue (RoD)
Confiteor
County people (see Tale of my Aunt Jenepher's wooing)
The Crown of Sheba's queen
A Daughter of the Medici (DoM)
The Day after to-morrow (HoI)

[50]

THE SHORT STORIES

Delilah, now it was dusk (Ch)
The Derby rule (*see* Tale of the gypsy horse)
Devised and bequeathed
Donoghu's hour (SwW)
Dramatis personae (Ch)
The Epistle to the Ephesians
Eve and the gopher
The Evil men do (DoM)
Executive session (AoFS)
The Fair girl of Wu (*see* Tale of my Uncle Cosimo)
Fantee
Fiddler's Green (HoI)
Fosterage (RoD)
Graft (RoD)
The Great gift (IoY)
Green eyes (*see* Mrs. Alexander Tyson)
Green isle (AoFS)
The Gryphon (IoY)
Hail and farewell (AoFS)
A Happy ending (DoM)
The Happy townland (AoFS)
Harley Johnston, gentleman (DoM)
Her last chance
His Honor The Court
Honorable of the earth (WoS)
The Hound of Ireland (HoI)
In a cellar (SwW)
In praise of James Carabine (*see* Tale of James Carabine)
In praise of Lady Margery (Ch)
An Infringement of the decalogue (WoS)
The Inseparables (*see* A Wife of no importance)
Inside stuff (*see* A Man's game)
"Irish" (Ch)
Irish gentility (*see* Tale of Kerry)
The Island of youth (IoY)
James Carabine's last fight (*see* Tale of James Carabine)
Jungle bulls (SwW)
The Keeper of the bridge (Ch)
Lazara (*see* The Supreme sacrifice)
The Lion in the streets (IoY)
London nights
A Man's game (SwW)
A Manner of legacy (IoY)
A Marriage has been arranged (WoS)

The Master of Raymond Lully (AoFS)
The Meditations of Kerry Macfarlane (DB)
The Miracle of Bethesda (IoY)
Mrs. Alexander Tyson (WoS)
Mrs. Dutton intervenes (HoI)
The Night of the Black Mass
The Night of Colonel Cray, retired
The Night of the dancer in red
The Night of O'Donnell Pasha
The Night of the profligate poet
The Night of the singing priest
O Snowy-breasted pearl (WoS)
One noose (*see* All three in one noose)
One woman
Out of Egypt (SwW)
Panic (SwW)
The Parable of the Bad Samaritan (IoY)
The Parliament at Thebes (Ch)
Patrick Leary's son
Paul and Ruth and Solomon (*see* Treachery)
The People of the state of New York (*see* The Day after to-morrow)
People of unimportance (*see* What became of Margot Gilholme)
Pipes o' glory (*see* Fosterage)
The Portrait of Marion Long (IoY)
The Prodigal in Utopia
Puppets of fate
The Purling brook which is Bow Sing Low's
A Quatrain of Ling Tai Fu's (Ch)
Reynardine (Ch)
Rivers of Damascus (RoD)
A Rubai of El Khayyam's (*see* The Evil men do)
The Ruby rose
The Rumbling drum (*see* The Evil men do)
Sargasso Sea (WoS)
Sea change (RoD)
Sentiment (HoI)
Sinister hand
The Sister act (*see* A Manner of legacy)
A Sister of shining swords (AoFS)
Slaves of the gun (SwW)
Sorrentina (*see* under Cinematizations)

The Sound of millstones (RoD)
Spanish Men's Rest (*see* Tale of my Cousin Jenico)
Steering-gear
A Story against women (Ch)
The Story of Suleyman Bey (SwW)
Superdirigible "Gamma-1" (IoY)
The Supreme sacrifice
Sweet honey in all mouths
Tale of the Chinese woman (*see* Tale of my Uncle Cosimo)
Tale of Golfer Gilligan (DB)
Tale of the gypsy horse (DB)
Tale of James Carabine (DB)
Tale of Kerry (DB)
Tale of my Aunt Jenepher's wooing (DB)
Tale of my Cousin Jenico at Spanish Men's Rest (DB)
Tale of my Uncle Cosimo and the fair girl of Wu (DB)
Tale of the piper (DB)
Tale told in Destiny Bay (DB)
Telepathy (*see* The Great gift)

The Thing called gratitude (RoD)
Through "Hell" to peace
Towers of silence (AoFS)
Treachery (AoFS)
A Treasure upon earth
Triangle (WoS)
Two who were thieves (*see* Bow Sing Low and the two who were thieves)
Underseaboat F-33 (HoI)
The Wake (SwW)
The Wall that is high (*see* Tale of Kerry)
What became of Margot Gilholme (WoS)
A Wife of no importance (RoD)
The Wife of the red-haired man (WoS)
Wisdom buildeth her house (Ch)
The Woman God changed (*see* Changeling)
A Woman in the house (RoD)
A Woman of the shee (WoS)
The Wrestler from Aleppo (WB)

Miscellaneous Writings
(IN APPROXIMATE CHRONOLOGICAL ORDER)

1. A notebook of holograph poems, written for Miss Dorothea May Cadogan (later Mrs. Donn Byrne) when both she and the author were students at the National University, Dublin.

This notebook is still in the possession of Mrs. Donn Byrne. It contains some dozen poems of varying length; several sonnets, a villanelle, and a number of longer poems, one "From the German of F. Linhard" and another "From the French of Henry (sic) Bataille." These probably represent the author's first attempts at verse. The following are the only ones known to have been published subsequently:

a. Villanelle. *The National student*, Dublin, May, 1910, p. 19. Signed "B."

b. Sonnet. *The National student*, Dublin, May, 1910, p. 9. Signed "B."

Both of the above are reproduced in Mr. Greenberg's *The tragedy of Donn Byrne*.

2. Other contributions to *The National student*.

This periodical was founded while Donn Byrne was an undergraduate at University College, and volume 1, no. 1, appeared under the date of May, 1910. A most interesting account of the inception of the journal appears in the issue of April, 1944 (new series, no. 89, p. 9f.); this article states that Bernard Byrne was one of the twelve undergraduates who met, "some time in the Hilary term of 1910," to launch the new venture. A personal communication from one of these twelve confirms the statement therein contained that it was Byrne himself who suggested the title of the journal. He is listed as a member of the editorial staff in the first issue only; shortly after its appearance, he graduated and left for the continent.

In addition to the "Sonnet" and "Villanelle" mentioned in "No. 1" above, the same issue contains an account of a paper which Byrne read at a meeting of the Literary and Historical Society; the subject was "Walt Whitman," and the paper itself is stated to have been "the most brilliant" of the 1909–1910 season.

In the issue of December, 1911, on p. 28, there appears a "Wedding Song," "dedicated, without permission, to B. Byrne, Esq." and dealing facetiously with his recent marriage in America.

It is possible that other material by Byrne appeared in the early issues, but to date none has been identified as his. In this connection, the following anthology may be of interest: Eimar O'Duffy, editor, *A college chorus. A collection of humorous verse by students of University College from the pages of "St. Stephen's" and "The National student."* Dublin: Martin Lester, Ltd., no date. The volume includes verses which appeared in student publications during the period when Byrne was an undergraduate; all of the poems are signed with pen names. While none of the verse has been attributed definitely to Byrne, the reference is cited here because of the possibility that some of it may have been his, and at some future date may be so identified.

3. Contributions to various newspapers, dictionaries, etc., including three editorials for the New York *Globe*, written mostly during the years 1911–1913, shortly after his arrival in New York. Most of this material, if not all of it, was

written anonymously, and none has been definitely identified to date. There are many references to this early "hack work," but none sufficiently detailed to permit exactitude in identification. See: Macauley, p. 28, 29, 42ff., etc.; *Bookman*, New York, 69:2, p. 152–157, April, 1929, McCardell, *New York Morning telegraph*, April 22, 1923; Greenberg, p. 26ff.

4. A poem about the San Francisco earthquake, said to have been published in *The United Irishman*, under the editorship of Arthur Griffith, ? date. See: Malone, *Dublin magazine*, October – December, 1928, p. 29; Malone, *America*, 39:17, p. 404, August 5, 1928; Malone, *Donn Byrne, an Irish realist*, London: Sampson Low, 1929, p. 28.

5. Contributions to *The Irish Republic*. None of these has been identified; the only known reference to them is in the McCardell reference cited under "3" above.

6. Contributions to *The Irish American*. This was a New York weekly, edited by Anthony J. Brogan during Donn Byrne's early Brooklyn days, which published a great deal of early writing by Mr. Byrne. As much of the journal's contents was unsigned, definite identification of all of the Donn Byrne material is out of the question, but the following is at least a partial list:

    a. 65:3, p. 5; January 18, 1913. Poem, "A ballad of Irish captains," signed by Bryan Donn-Byrne.

    b. 65:4, p. 5; January 25, 1913. "A treasury of Irish legendry," signed by Bryan Donn-Byrne. A review of Rolleston's *Myths and legends of the Irish race*.

    c. 65:7, p. 4; February 15, 1913. "The printed word." A signed column, reviewing several books, among them James Stephens' *The crock of gold*.

    d. 65:10, p. 4; March 8, 1913. "The printed word." More book reviews; probably by Donn Byrne, but not signed.

    e. 65:27, p. 4; July 5, 1913. "Without prejudice" (signed column). Also, same page, column of reviews, "From our book shelf," possibly by Donn Byrne.

    f. 65:28, p. 4; July 12, 1913; "Without prejudice" (signed column). Also, possibly by Byrne, book review column signed "Eoghan."

    g. 65:30, p. 4; July 26, 1913. "Without prejudice."

    h. 65:31, p. 4; August 2, 1913. "Without prejudice." Also, on same page, unsigned but possibly by Byrne, a column entitled "Art, poetry, and shindigs."

    i. 65:31, p. 5; August 2, 1913. Signed letter, in praise of Douglas Hyde.

    j. 65:35, p. 4; August 30, 1913 "Midsummer madness." A signed letter, on the topic of writing letters to New York newspapers in defense of Ireland.

    k. 65:36, p. 4; September 6, 1913. Editorial "An old friend departs," unsigned but probably by Donn Byrne.

    l. 65:38, p. 4; September 20, 1913. "The passing of Big Tim." Signed, Bryan Donn-Byrne.

This periodical doubtless contains a great deal of additional writing by Donn Byrne, but none has been definitely identified as his. In addition, there are many accounts of meetings of various Irish organizations, The Irish Scholars Club of

MISCELLANEOUS WRITINGS

Brooklyn, The Brooklyn Gaelic Society, etc., etc. Lists of attendees at these meetings are frequently given, and the name Byrne appears often, but with no identifying given name or initial.

7. Contributions to *The Philippine bulletin*.

Donn Byrne was editor of this periodical from its inception in July, 1913, through December of the same year. None of the six issues published during this period contain anything over his signature, but it is probable that much if not all of the unsigned material was written by him. Lacking means of positive identification, the following articles seem among those most likely to have come from his pen:

a. 1:1; July, 1913. "The clearing house." A series of short articles dealing with various aspects of Philippine commerce, arts and crafts, agriculture, education, etc. Also, in the same issue, the account of the first annual dinner of the Philippine Society, held June 10, 1913, at the Hotel Plaza.

b. 1:4; October, 1913. An editorial dealing with the Philippine vocabulary as covered in Dr. F. H. Vizetelly's *New standard dictionary*. As Donn Byrne worked on this project with Dr. Vizetelly, it is extremely likely that he was responsible for inclusion of this particular article.

c. 1:5; November, 1913. Editorial entitled "A Filipino white hope," dealing with Francisco Labra, a pugilist visiting the United States to take part in prizefights. Donn Byrne's well-known interest in the ring seems likely to have been responsible for this piece of writing. In the same issue, a review entitled "Commander Porter's latest book" (*The Streak*, by David Porter; Philadelphia: J. B. Lippincott, 1913). The style of this review so closely parallels that of the signed reviews in *The Irish American* that it can almost certainly be attributed to Donn Byrne.

8. Poem, "All things having strange beauty." Two quatrains in typescript, property of the Library of Congress. Undated, and date and place of publication, if any, unknown.

9. "Down by the tan-yard side." A very short one-act play, an incomplete galley proof of which is in the Library of Congress. It is marked "Copyright, January, 1914," but the L. of C. "List of dramatic compositions" copyrighted through 1916 does not include this title. There is no available information as to whether or not this little play was ever performed or published.

10. "Laurette Taylor." An interview, published in *The Delineator*, July, 1914 (85:1, p. 13).

11. A personal communication from the late Achmed Abdullah, written shortly before his death, contains the following statement: "The late Donn Byrne, whom I first met in his native Brooklyn, and I worked together on about a half dozen stories which, by this time, have been drowned in the sea of pulp." He goes on to say that some of these were published under his own name, and some under that of Donn Byrne. It seems unfortunately likely that the passage of time and the decease of both writers will prevent the eventual identification, by author, of these tales. The only other clue, which in itself may be misleading, is Mr. Abdullah's further statement that "their milieu was laid in Africa."

DONN BYRNE BIBLIOGRAPHY

12. *New York Times*, VIII, 276:1; May 11, 1919. The letter in defense of Theodore Dreiser's *Twelve men*, quoted in part in Mr. Macauley's biography, p. 67.

13. Williams, Blanche Colton, *How to study "The best short stories,"* New York: Small, Maynard, 1919. On p. 43, in discussing the short story "The wake," Miss Williams quotes at some length from a personal communication written her by Donn Byrne. In addition to this particular story, the letter mentions also "Sargasso Sea" and "A treasure upon earth."

14. Original scenario, "Sorrentina" (1920). See under "Cinematizations."

15. Original scenario, "Moon of Persia" (1920). See under "Cinematizations."

16. *New York Times*, VI, 4:2; April 4, 1920. The Joseph Anthony interview, quoted very extensively by Mr. Macauley and others, giving Donn Byrne's views on novels, novelists, and novel-writing. Title, "Donn Byrne on literary buccaneering."

17. *Century magazine*, "Among our contributors" column, issues of December, 1921, and April and May, 1922. Comment by Donn Byrne on his story, "Wisdom buildeth her house."

18. *Bookman*, New York, 55:4, p. 351–353; June, 1922. "Five poems from the Gaelic," with an introduction, by Donn Byrne.

19. Excerpts from a letter to his former secretary, Miss Davids, written from Greythorn (Dun Laoghaire) and dated January 3, 1923; reproduced in Mr. Greenberg's *Tragedy of Donn Byrne*.

20. Schnittkind and Baker, *Best college stories*. Boston: Stratford, 1925. Pages 353–354 contain, as part of a symposium on "How I have attained literary success," a brief account by Donn Byrne of his methods of writing and marketing his stories.

21. A brief letter alleged to have been written by Donn Byrne, to Commissioner O'Byrne in 1926, in response to a summons to report for jury duty. This letter is mentioned in the *New York Times* of June 22, 1928 (25:5), and also in Mr. Greenberg's thesis. The handwriting is Mrs. Donn-Byrne's rather than that of her husband, and the letter was probably dictated by him.

22. *Daily Mail*, London, 20 June 1928. "Donn Byrne, by himself."

23. Various letters, quotations from letters, personal quotations, etc., many of which are not generally available, and which for the sake of convenience are grouped together in the following miscellany:

  a. Verbal and written material cited by Mr. Macauley in his biography, p. 3ff., 14, 20f., 24, 26, 30f., 40, 44f., 59, 114, 118ff., 122, 129, 144f., 156ff., 170, 174, 181, 187, 189, 191ff., 206f.

  b. Large collections of personal communications, collected letters, association material, etc., in the possession of Mrs. Donn-Byrne, Miss Georgina Davids, Mr. O. K. Liveright, and others, including the compiler of this bibliography.

MISCELLANEOUS WRITINGS

c. *New York World*, June 22, 1928. "The first reader," by Harry Hansen, quotes Donn Byrne's alleged views on newspaper and magazine editors.

d. Decca Record Co., Ltd., London. Brochure, issued January, 1934, quotes Donn Byrne regarding the records of Mr. H. Richard Hayward: "The most hearteningly beautiful things of their kind in the world."

e. *Bookman*, New York, 52:6, p. 572. Quotation from letter; 55:3, p. 330, May, 1922, as above; 61:6, p. 729, August, 1925. Quotes Donn Byrne on *Blind Raftery*.

f. *Pictorial review*, 30:8, p. 1; May, 1929. "I consider 'Field of honor' the finest story I have ever written."

g. *Collier's magazine*, 72:23, p. 38; December 8, 1923. "I think it's [A story against women] by far the best short story I've ever done."

h. Quotation from an unidentified obituary article: "Don't ask me what about England. I'm utterly Irish, and I don't know what about England. But we have freed Ireland and now will try to free England. We Irish writers will free England. It needs freeing. We use our freedom in Ireland backing losing race horses and losing hands at bridge." (This was evidently quoted from a newspaper interview with Donn Byrne on the occasion of his visit to America in 1925. See *New York Times*, June 10, 1925; 14:2.)

i. *New York Evening post*, June 11, 1925, p. 14. Extensive interview, with much material directly quoted.

j. *New York Sun*, June 17, 1925, p. 36. Same comment as above.

k. *New York Telegram-Mail*, June 24, 1925. As above.

l. Publicity releases in connection with the William Fox production of the *Hangman's House* motion picture; quotation from a letter written to John Ford, who directed the film: "The writing of this novel gave me the greatest satisfaction of my literary career. I hope you will find equal pleasure in filming it."

m. ALS inserted in a copy of *Hangman's House* sold at auction by Ritter Hopson Galleries, Newark, N. J., November 11, 1930, and described in their catalogue no. 6.

n. *Boston*, Mass., *Post*, October 15, 1922. Donn Byrne quoted regarding his advice to young authors. This article also speaks of Donn Byrne as the author of "those famous short stories, 'The keeper of the bridge' and 'Puppets of fate.'" The magazine appearance of this latter story has not been located (see note under Cinematizations — the scenario entitled "Sorrentina").

24. There are numerous discrepancies between the magazine and book versions of almost all of the stories, and even, in many instances, between the texts of the English and American volumes. Most of these variations are insignificant in that they have to do with differences in spelling, punctuation, and the like. Of more than minor interest, however, are the many changes in phraseology, the substitutions of one word for another, the addition or deletion of relatively long passages, which occur in connection with some of the stories.

A complete table of these would require more space than is available in a compilation such as this; as a compromise, however, for those who are anxious to read "everything that Donn Byrne ever wrote," the following list of titles will be found to include those stories the manuscript or magazine versions of which differ materially from the text of the book appearance, or in which the differences are particularly numerous, interesting, or lengthy: Bow Sing Low and the two who were thieves, "Irish," A quatrain of Ling Tai Fu's, Blue waves of Tory, The meditations of Kerry MacFarlane, Tale of my Aunt Jenepher's wooing, Tale of my Uncle Cosimo and the fair girl of Wu, Tale of the gypsy horse, Triangle, A brevity on page three, An infringement of the decalogue, The happy townland.

25. Although not belonging, strictly speaking, under the heading of "Miscellaneous Writing," there are listed below some of the uncompleted or projected works of Donn Byrne, none of which ever reached the stage of publication:

a. A novel, to be called "The case is altered." (See Mr. Macauley's biography, p. 190; *Bookman*, New York, April, 1929, p. 156.)

b. A book about the horse. (See Macauley, p. 190.)

c. An autobiography. (See Macauley, p. 191, and "27" below.)

d. A play. (See *Bookman*, New York, 55:4, p. 449; June, 1922.)

e. "The house of gold." (See *Century magazine*, 104:1, adv.; May, 1922; "Among our contributors" column.) Presumably this was an early title for the book published as *Blind Raftery*, but it is mentioned here on the chance that it was another book which was started but not finished.

f. A story about Madame Blavatsky, told as a "Dramatic poem." (See *New York Post*, March 4, 1922.)

g. See letter to Blanche Colton Williams, quoted under "Destiny Bay."

26. See Appendix, Note 1 (inscribed presentation copies).

27. In connection with No. 25c, above, it may be of some interest to quote from a letter written by Donn Byrne to a friend in America. The letter is dated from Coolmain Castle 27 June, 1927, and reads in part as follows: "Ten years from now, when I have a long beard flecked with grey, reaching to the fourth button of my waistcoat, and sufficient money in the bank to provide for myself, wife and young, I shall sit down and write a long-winded, dreary, egotistical autobiography, which perhaps somebody will read out of sheer curiosity, to think that such things can be . . ."

28. Original scenario, "Parnell." (See under "Cinematizations.")

29. In some biographical notes, prepared by Miss Georgina Davids under Donn Byrne's supervision, around 1920, there are listed the following academic distinctions at University College, Dublin: Medalist in Gaelic Verse; O'Curry Prize Man in Gaelic Literature; Medalist in English Verse; King's Scholar in English Literature; Bishop's Scholar in Romance Languages.

The writings which gained the author these honors have not been identified, but it is quite possible that they may be on file at University College.

30. Mr. Thomas J. Tiernan of Chicago is authority for the statement that "Donn Byrne is said to have written for *The Playboy*." (This was a "little magazine" published in New York City, 1919–1924.)

Translations

1. A personal communication from Messrs. Sampson Low, Marston & Co., Ltd., dated 18 February 1944, states, in part: "In 1926 we entered into arrangements for the translation of 'Changeling' and 'Messer Marco Polo' into Polish, but are unable to say whether these titles were actually published. In 1930 arrangements were made for the translation and publication in the Italian language of the 13 titles already published by us. The titles, so far as we can discover, were:

An Untitled Story
Blind Raftery
Brother Saul
Changeling
Crusade
Destiny Bay
The Foolish Matrons

The Golden Goat
Hangman's House
Ireland, the Rock, etc.
Messer Marco Polo
Power of the Dog
The Wind Bloweth

We are unable to confirm what titles were published in the Irish language, and cannot trace any others that were published in French, only the title mentioned by you." (This latter reference is to "Destiny Bay," q. v., below.)

2. The following titles have been translated into Irish, and published by The Stationery Office, Dublin: Hangman's House (1935); Messer Marco Polo (1938); The power of the dog (1940).

3. *Brother Saul*. Broder Saul. Oversat af Knud Hee Andersen. Aarhus, 1932. 254 p.

4. *Destiny Bay*. La Baie du Destin. Tr. par Maurice Rances. Paris: Librairie Gallimard, éds. de la Nouvelle Revue Française, 1931. Paper, 12 x 19 cm., p. 315. Fr. 15.
    This volume contains five of the Destiny Bay stories. A very interesting review by André Bellesort appeared in the *Correspondant*, Paris, January 10, 1932, p. 138–146. Other reviews in the French periodical press have not been located.
    La Baia del Destino: traduzione di Ada Salvatori. Roma: Editoriale Romana [1944]. 314 p. 19 cm. (Collezione "Alfa." [3.])

5. *Hangman's House*. Det stora grå huset. Roman fran Irland. Oversattning av Karl Ekman. Stockholm, 1928. 364 p. 8°.
    First published in *Hvar 8 dag*, 28:9, p. 24–26; 10, p. 23–26; 11, p. 23–26; 12, p. 23–26; 13, p. 19–22; 14, p. 19–22; 15, p. 19–22; 16, p. 19–22; 17, p. 19–22; 18, p. 19–22; 19, p. 19–22; 20, p. 23–26; 21, p. 19–22; 22, p. 19–22; 23, p. 19–22; 24, p. 23–26; 25, p. 19–22; 26, p. 23–26; 27, p. 23–26; 28, p. 23–26; 29, p. 23–26; 30, p. 23–26; Nov. 28, 1926 – April 24, 1927.

6. *Messer Marco Polo*. Maese Marco Polo. Traducción directa del inglés y nota prologal de Jack Davidson. Buenos Aires: Editorial Ayacucho [1945]. 4 p.l., 11–127 p., 1 l., illus. 19 cm. ([Colección moderna; novelas cortas. 3.])

7. In describing the Metts presentation copy of *Stories without women*, the American Art Association-Anderson Galleries catalogue no. 4201 (November 13-14, 1935) states that there are pencilled notes in the volume indicating that certain of the stories have been translated. No further details are given, and the present writer has not had an opportunity to inspect this particular copy, so that the particular titles translated, and into what language or languages, is at present undetermined.

8. It is extremely likely that many of the short stories and novels of Donn Byrne have appeared in translations not mentioned above. It is extremely unlikely that there will ever be available complete data concerning them. Many of the periodicals in which the early stories appeared have long since ceased publication, and their records are no longer in existence. Publishers and literary agents in this country disclaim knowledge of any such translations. Messrs. Sampson Low, who at one time had a fairly complete record of this information, were "bombed out" four times during the years 1940–1945, and in one of the visitations all of their files, correspondence, and records of every description were completely destroyed. An indefatigable bibliographer with a working knowledge of most of the Continental languages, and unlimited time at his disposal, could probably turn up details concerning a large body of Byrniana published in many parts of Europe; the compiler has even heard rumors, which he has not been able to verify, concerning translations into Chinese and Japanese.

9. The following titles have been done into Braille:

a. Messer Marco Polo. Service for the Blind, Library of Congress, Perkins Institution and Massachusetts School for the Blind, Watertown, Massachusetts; Wisconsin School for the Blind, Janesville, Wisconsin.

b. Blind Raftery. Library of Congress.

c. Island of youth. Iowa Commission for the Blind, Des Moines.

d. Hangman's House. Wisconsin.

e. The Wind bloweth. Wisconsin.

f. Changeling. Perkins Institution.

g. Brother Saul. Perkins Institution.

h. Ireland. Perkins Institution.

Other editions of Donn Byrne's books, transcribed by hand into Braille, are distributed in various libraries in the United States, and include the following titles: Blind Raftery, Crusade, Destiny Bay, The fair girl of Wu, Hangman's House, A party of baccarat, The wind bloweth, and O'Malley of Shanganagh.

Most of the above data is furnished through the courtesy of the Messrs. D. Appleton-Century Co., and Miss Ruth M. Knapp, Assistant Librarian, Perkins Institution and Massachusetts School for the Blind. As new titles are constantly being added, the list as presented above is probably incomplete at the present time.

Anthologies

1. The lyric year. Edited by Ferdinand Earle. New York: Mitchell Kennerley, 1912.

This anthology of verse contains "The piper" (p. 28–29), and also (p. 301) a biographical sketch of the author, probably the first to appear in print. His name is given as "Bryan *(sic)* Oswald Donn-Byrne," and year of birth is stated to be 1885. Further mention includes the statement that he is Secretary of the Gaelic Literature Association of America.

2. Best short stories of 1915. Edited by Edward J. O'Brien. Boston: Small, Maynard, 1916.

Contains "The wake" (p. 35–45). Many contemporary reviews single out this story for special mention. See *New York Times book review*, May 21, 1916, p. 215.

3. War stories. Edited by R. J. Holmes and A. Starbuck. New York: Crowell, 1919.

Contains "Underseaboat F-33" (p. 61–78). One of the numerous reviews which mention this story specifically is that in the *Boston Evening Transcript*, July 2, 1919; II:8, col. 7.

An accompanying biographical sketch (p. 324) gives the author's birth date as 1888, the year of his Dublin degree as 1909, and mentions his athletic and sporting interests.

4. Masterpieces of adventure. Edited by Nella Braddy. New York: Doubleday, Page, 1921, 1927.

Vol. 3, p. 73–97, "Superdirigible 'Gamma-1'."

5. Good stories. Edited by Frank Luther Mott. New York: Macmillan, 1936.

"Tale of James Carabine."

6. "Dawgs." Edited by Charles W. Gray. New York: Holt, 1925.

"Triangle." Among reviews making specific reference to this story are *Boston Evening Transcript*, October 10, 1925, Book section, 4:6; *New York Herald Tribune books*, November 15, 1925, VI:9, col. 5.

7. Real dogs. Edited by Charles W. Gray. New York: Holt, 1926.

"The Hound of Ireland." Story is briefly mentioned in most of the reviews of this book. See *Boston Evening Transcript*, December 8, 1926, Book section, 6:5–6.

This volume is dedicated to Donn Byrne.

8. "Hosses." Edited by Charles W. Gray. New York: Holt, 1927.

Pages 91–124, "A story against women." Among reviews mentioning this specific story are *Saturday review of literature*, 4:7, 108, September 10, 1927; *New York Times book review*, August 28, 1927, p. 16; *Boston Evening Transcript*, November 12, 1927, Book section, 7:6.

DONN BYRNE BIBLIOGRAPHY

9. The Omnibus of sport. Edited by Grantland Rice and Harford Powel. Illustrated by Lee Townsend. New York: Harper's, 1932.

Pages 692–720, "Rivers of Damascus." Story is mentioned briefly in most of the reviews; see *New York Herald Tribune books*, x:8, August 7, 1932.

10. Short narratives. Edited by Paul M. Fulcher. New York: Century, 1928.

Pages 49–57, "The wrestler from Aleppo."

11. The Smart Set anthology. Edited by Burton Rascoe and Groff Conklin. New York: Reynal and Hitchcock, 1934.

Contains the poems "Reveil" (p. 409) and "The kingdom of Thule" (p. 601). Brief mention in many reviews, as for example *Saturday review of literature*, 11:20, p. 326, December 1, 1934; *New York Times book review*, December 9, 1934, p. 2.

12. Boxing in art and literature. Edited by William D. Cox. New York: Reynal and Hitchcock, 1935.

Pages 172–189, "Tale of James Carabine" (incomplete version). Typical reviews include the following: *New York Herald Tribune books*, vii:21, October 6, 1935, and *New York Times book review*, September 8, 1935, p. 2.

13. The sportsman's anthology. Edited by R. F. Kelley. New York: Howell, Soskin, 1944.

"Tale of the gypsy horse."

14. Treasury of animal stories. Edited by C. L. Mally. New York: Citadel Press, 1946.

"Tale of the gypsy horse."

15. Readings in contemporary literature, by Ernest Hanes and Martha Jane McCoy. New York: Macmillan, 1928.

Pages 102–109, "The wake."

Dramatizations

Hangman's House.

Play of same title, in four acts, dramatized by Willard Mack and produced by William A. Brady, jr., and Dwight Deere Wiman. Opened at Forrest Theatre, New York, on December 16, 1926, and ran for eight performances.

Reviews and other references: Burns Mantle, *Best plays of 1926–27,* p. 441–442; *Life,* 89:2305, p. 21, January 6, 1927 (Robert Benchley); *Time,* 8:26, p. 30, December 27, 1926; *Judge,* 92:2358, p. 16, January 8, 1927 (George Jean Nathan); *New York Herald Tribune,* December 18, 1926, p. 14, col. 2–3 (Percy Hammond); *New York Times,* December 17, 1926, p. 27, col. 2 (J. Brooks Atkinson); *New York Herald Tribune,* December 19, 1926, VI:4, cols. 3–4.

Messer Marco Polo.

  a. Dramatization by Louise Harley. *World review,* Mt. Morris, Ill., 4:74–75, March 7, 1927. This is not strictly speaking a play, but rather a condensed version or sort of scenario to be used as the basis of a play for school use. Whether or not it was subsequently adapted and used as such has not been determined.

  b. Dramatization by A. Herbert Greenberg. This has not been produced or published. Details concerning it will be found in Mr. Greenberg's thesis, p. 102.

  c. Dramatization by Harry Wagstaff Gribble. Never produced or published. References to Mr. Gribble's play appear in the *New York Times,* September 8, 1924, and in Mr. Greenberg's thesis, p. 106.

  d. Radio dramatization. Broadcast over NBC Red Network, November 12, 1929, at 9.00 P.M. Personal communications from officials of the NBC give no details as to the authorship of this radio version, but state that the cast was headed by Allyn Joslyn and Rosaline Green, and that music was furnished by the Eveready Orchestra.

Blind Raftery.

Radio dramatization by Edwina Sedgewick, broadcast over the British Broadcasting Co. Home Service Program, 15 February 1945, at 9.30 P.M.

Down by the tanyard side.

This, strictly speaking, is not a dramatization of one of the stories, but rather a short one-act play written by Donn Byrne himself. Only details known are those given under Miscellaneous Writings, no. 9.

Cinematizations

Fiddlers' Green.

Motion picture based on above story, dramatized by Garfield Thompson, and re-titled "All man." A Vitagraph production, in five reels, directed by Paul Scardon, starring Harry Morey and Betty Blythe.

Reviews. Moving picture world, August 17, 1918, p. 1015; *Film daily,* August 4, 1918; *Variety,* 51:10, p. 39, August 2, 1918.

A prodigal in Utopia.

Scenario by C. G. Sullivan. Directed by Fred Niblo and produced by Thomas H. Ince. Federal copyright no. 326639 (Los Angeles). Released 1919 (?). No further details known.

The bride of Kenmore.

Reference is made to a motion picture of this title, in a letter from the International Magazine Co., dated March 24, 1921. No picture of this title has been located, and, as it was in *Hearst's international* that "The bride's play" appeared as a short story, it seems more than likely that the reference is to the cinematization of this story.

Moon of Persia.

In the Wetherbee Collection there is an original scenario by Donn Byrne, bearing this title, and dated at Riverside, "Noel, 1920." Whether or not it was ever filmed has not been determined.

Ghosts of glory.

Also in the Wetherbee Collection is a copy of a telegram from Donn Byrne to Bayard Veiller, congratulating him on the picture "Puppets of fate," and inquiring about another with the above title. No record of a motion picture of this name has been located to date. Possibly it refers to a motion picture version of the story "Pipes o' glory," which, again, has not been identified.

Sorrentina.

Motion picture title, "Puppets of fate." A synopsis of this story, in thirty-six typewritten pages, is in the Wetherbee Collection. A personal communication from Mr. Edward Hogan, of the Metro-Goldwyn-Mayer Story Department, states that this was written to order by Donn Byrne, and that it never appeared as a short story in any periodical. Miss Davids, Mr. Byrne's former secretary, writes that according to her recollection, the story did appear in some magazine, under the title "Sorrentina," but that she is unable to recall which one. (See Miscellaneous writings, 23n.)

The synopsis was purchased by Metro for $8,000, the contract bearing the date 11 October 1920. Produced by Metro; scenario by Ruth Ann Baldwin and Molly Parro; directed by Dallas M. Fitzgerald; photographed by John Arnold; art director, Sidney Ullman. Six reels, released March 28, 1921. Featured players, Viola Dana and Francis McDonald.

Reviews. Moving picture world, 49:9, p. 992, April 30, 1921; *Variety*, 62:9, p. 40, April 22, 1921; *Life*, 77.2007, p. 576, April 21, 1921.

Changeling (1).

Motion picture title, "The woman God changed." Produced by Famous Players-Lasky (Paramount), a Cosmopolitan production. Photoplay by D. Hobart; director, R. G. Vignola; seven reels. Featured players, Seena Owen and E. K. Lincoln. Released May, 1921.

Reviews and other references: Film daily, June 5, 1921; *Variety*, May 27, 1921; *Photoplay magazine*, 20.1, p. 35–38, 100–102, June, 1921; *Life*, August 4, 1921, p. 29; *Hearst's international*, January, 1921, p. 2, *Moving picture world*, May 7, 1921, p. 13–16; *ibid.*, June 4, 1921, p. 538; *Cosmopolitan*, 61:4, p. 50, October, 1921; *Exceptional photoplays*, 1:5, May, 1921; *New Yorker*, 16:31, p. 61–68, September 14, 1940 (M. R. Werner, "That was New York. Yellow movies." Account of Mr. Werner's association with Cosmopolitan Productions in 1921, with details concerning the filming of this story and of "The bride's play"); *The Film index, a bibliography*, Vol. I, The Film as Art, p. 417.

The foolish matrons.

Motion picture of same title. Associated Producers; directed by Maurice Tourneur; scenario by Wyndham Gittens; photography by Charles van Enger and K. G. MacLean. Six reels. Featured players, Hobart Bosworth and Doris May.

Reviews and other references: Film daily, July 3, 1921; *Moving picture world*, July 2, 1921, p. 114; *Boston Sunday Advertiser*, July 10, 1921, 6E:6.

According to Mr. Macauley (p. 65, Century edition) Donn Byrne received $10,000 each for the film rights to this novel and "The strangers' banquet."

The bride's play.

Motion picture of same title. Produced by Famous Players-Lasky (Paramount), a Cosmopolitan production. Seven reels. Director, George Terwilliger; scenarist, Mildred Considine; settings, Joseph Urban; photographer, Ira H. Morgan; cast headed by Marion Davies. Played Rialto Theatre, New York, week of January 8, 1922.

Reviews and other references: Film daily, January 15, 1922; *New York Times*, January 8, 1922; *Hearst's international*, April, 1922 (photograph); *Boston American*, March 6, 1922, 9:4–5; *Moving picture world*, January 21, 1922, p. 320; *New York Telegraph*, January 15, 1922; *New Yorker*, 16:31, p. 61–68, September 14, 1940 (M. R. Werner: "That was New York. Yellow movies." Account of Mr. Werner's association with Cosmopolitan Productions in 1921, with details concerning the making of this picture and "The woman God changed.").

The strangers' banquet.

Motion picture of same title, produced by Marshall Neilan and distributed by Goldwyn. Seven reels. Director, Marshall Neilan; cameramen, David Kesson and

M. Fabian; all-star cast, headed by Claire Windsor and Hobart Bosworth. Released December 31, 1922. Presented by S. L. Rothafel at Capitol Theatre, New York, week of January 1, 1923.

Reviews and other references: Film daily, January 7, 1923; *New York Times*, 18:1, January 1, 1923; *Variety*, January 5, 1923, p. 54; *Billboard*, January 6, 1923, p. 54; *New York Tribune*, January 1, 1923, 8:4–5; *Moving picture world*, January 6, 1923, p. 4–5; January 13, 1923, p. 154, *Metropolitan magazine*, 57:1, p. 41, April, 1923 (portrait); *Red book*, April, 1923 (portrait); *Washington, D. C., Post*, January 28, 1923; Scott Odell, *Representative photoplays*, 1924, p. 170–174 (synopsis and scenario analysis).

See also note under "The foolish matrons" regarding sale of film rights.

In praise of James Carabine.

Motion picture title, "Blarney." A Metro-Goldwyn-Mayer production, directed by Marcel de Sano, scenario by Albert Lewin, photography by Ben Reynolds. Six reels. Featured players, Renée Adorée, Paulette Duval, Ralph Graves.

Reviews and other references: Film daily, October 10, 1926; *Variety*, August 25, 1926, p. 23; *Chicago Herald and Examiner*, 19.1, September 24, 1926.

Hangman's House.

Motion picture of same title, produced by William Fox, directed by John Ford, scenario by Marion Orth, edited by Margaret V. Clancy, title writer, Malcolm Stuart Boylan, photography by George Schneidermann. Featured players, Victor Maclagan, June Collyer, Larry Kent, Earle Fox, and Hobart Bosworth. Played Roxy Theatre, New York, week of May 12, 1928.

Reviews and other references: Moving picture world, August 11, 1928, p. 96; *Film daily*, May 20, 1928; *Variety*, May 16, 1928, p. 13; *Billboard*, May 26, 1928, p. 24; *Life*, 91:2378, p. 23, May 31, 1928 (R. E. Sherwood); *New York Times*, IX, 5:4, May 13, 1928; 25:1, May 14, 1928; VIII, 5:1, May 20, 1928.

See also, "Miscellaneous Writings," no. 23–I.

Changeling (2).

Motion picture title, "His captive woman." A First National Vitaphone production, directed by George Fitzmaurice, scenario by Carey Wilson, photographed by Lee Garmes. Featured players, Dorothy Mackaill, Milton Sills, George Fawcett.

Reviews and other references: Film daily, April 7, 1929; *New York World*, June 16, 1929 (letter, Thurston Macauley); *New York Times*, 26:4, April 8, 1929; 10:7, 3, April 7, 1929; *Boston Transcript*, May 8, 1929; *Life*, 93:2428, p. 29–38, May 17, 1929 (H. Evans); *Outlook*, 152:3, p. 112, May 15, 1929 (A. M. Sherwood, jr.); *San Francisco Chronicle*, November 18, 1928; *Boston Herald*, May 7, 1929; 21:7–8.

Destiny Bay.

Motion picture title, "Wings of the morning." Twentieth Century-Fox; producer, Robert T. Kane; director, Harold Schuster; screen play, Tom Geraghty;

CINEMATIZATIONS

color director, Natalie Kalmus, photographer, Ray Rennahan, music, Arthur Benjamin; art director, Ralph Brinton; costumes, Irene Herbert; editor, James Clark; cameramen, Henry Imus, Jack Cardiff. Released February 19, 1937. Played Radio City Music Hall, New York, week of March 11, 1937. Featured players, Annabella and Henry Fonda.

Reviews and other references: Liberty, February 13, 1937, p. 53, *Movie story,* March, 1937; *Billboard,* March 20, 1937; *Variety,* March 17, 1937, p. 14; *Time,* 29.9, p. 65, March 1, 1937; *Motion picture magazine,* April, 1937; *Boston Herald,* March 13, 1937, March 18, 1937; *New York Herald-Tribune,* March 12, 1937; *New York Times,* March 12, 1937, p. 19, *Literary digest,* 123:12, p. 28, March 20, 1937; *Hollywood spectator,* February 13, 1937, p. 12; *Film daily,* February 2, 1937, p. 7; *Motion picture guide,* April, 1937; *Motion picture review,* March, 1937; *Christian Science monitor,* March 27, 1937, p. 15; *New York Sun,* March 12, 1937, p. 35; *New York World Telegram,* March 12, 1937, p. 38, *New Yorker,* March 20, 1937, p. 93; *Boston Traveler,* March 13, 1937; *Esquire,* April, 1937; *News-week,* March 27, 1937; *Fox West Coast bulletin,* February 13, 1937; *Weekly guide,* February 20, 1937; *Script,* February 13, 1937, p. 9; *Box office,* February 6, 1937, p. 23; *Hollywood reporter,* January 29, 1937, p. 3; *Variety,* Hollywood, January 29, 1937, p. 3; *Christian century,* March 24, 1937, p. 399; *Boston Globe,* March 13, 1937; *New statesman,* 13:848, May 22, 1937; *Illustrated London news,* 190:986, May 29, 1937; *Spectator,* 158:1091, June 11, 1937; *Theatre world,* 28:42, July, 1937; *Judge,* 112.2703, p. 21, June, 1937.

Parnell.

Motion picture scenario, written at Riverside (?1918), never sold. The only extant copy of this work is in possession of Miss Davids, Donn Byrne's former secretary.

General Reference List

A. References of Major Interest

1. Macauley, Thurston Donn Byrne, bard of Armagh. New York: Century, 1929; London: Sampson Low, 1929.

Biography containing many illustrations (these differ in American and English editions), quotations from letters and reviews, and an abbreviated bibliography. See also, by same author: (1a) Passport to Tir Nan Og. *Bookman*, New York, 69:2, p. 152-157, April, 1929. Subtitle: The life, work, and death of Donn Byrne. (1b) Donn Byrne's Ireland. *North American review*, 230:5, p. 605-609, November, 1930.

2. Greenberg, A. Herbert. The tragedy of Donn Byrne. Thesis submitted to Department of English, Columbia University, in partial fulfillment of requirements for M. A. degree, 1936.

This thesis is of particular importance in that it contains a great deal of information not previously available — well-documented details regarding the Byrne family, photographs of Donn Byrne's various residences, excerpts from letters by and about Donn Byrne, and photostatic reproductions of two of his earliest poems, published in *The National student*.

3. Rosenthal, Jacob. The literary sources of Donn Byrne's novels.

Like the above, a Columbia University M. A. thesis of 1936; Mr. Rosenthal is concerned with literary criticism rather than biography or bibliography, and while many readers may not agree with his conclusions, they have at least the merit of being provocative.

4. Wetherbee, Winthrop, Jr. (Brian Oswald) Donn Byrne. A bibliography. Boston: F. W. Faxon, 1938. (Bulletin of Bibliography pamphlets. no. 34.)

A preliminary bibliography. Reprinted from *Bulletin of bibliography*, nos. 145-150; September, 1937 – August, 1939.

5. Malone, Andrew E. Donn Byrne, an Irish realist. London: Sampson Low, 1929.

Well-illustrated brochure of 48 pages, appraising and eulogizing the life and works of Donn Byrne. See also, by same author: (5a) Donn Byrne: an appreciation. *America*, 39:17, p. 404-405, August 4, 1928; *Dublin magazine*, October – December, 1928, p. 21-35.

6. Adcock, A. St. John. Donn Byrne. A biographical sketch. London: Sampson Low, 1929.

An illustrated pamphlet, reviewing Donn Byrne's life and writings. See also, "9," below.

7. O'Connor, T. P. The genius of Donn Byrne. Mellon, Paul. Donn Byrne — his place in literature. New York: Century, 1929.

Pamphlet. The first article is reprinted from *T. P.'s weekly* (October 31, 1925); the second is a prize Yale literary essay.

GENERAL REFERENCE LIST

8. Metcalfe, Cranstoun. Donn Byrne. *Bookman*, London, 71:422, p. 101–103, November, 1926.
Sketch, illustrated with the E. Brooks Hughes photograph.

9. Adcock, A. St. John. Gods of modern Grub Street. New York: Stokes, 1923, p. 51–60, also, London: Sampson Low, 1924.
Sketch, illustrated with the E. O. Hoppé photograph.

10. Baldwin, C. C. The men who make our novels. New York: Dodd, Mead, 1924, p. 71–73.
Sketch, of special interest because of its disparaging attitude towards Donn Byrne both as an individual and as a writer.

11. Downey, John J. Some objections to the novels of Donn Byrne. *Catholic world*, 128:767, p. 566–570, February, 1929.
Further disparagement of Donn Byrne, chiefly on grounds of apostasy.

12. Haywood, H. Richard. An Irish novelist. *Ulster review*, ? date.
This reference is cited by Mr. Macauley, who gives no further identifying details. A personal communication from Mr. Haywood states that he too is unable to furnish the date of the article, and that the periodical in question ceased publication years ago. He adds that there was nothing in this article which was not included in Mr. Macauley's book. See also, by same author: (12a) Donn Byrne, an Ulster novelist. *Northern Whig*, Belfast, 16 August 1924.

13. Millis, Walter. The legend of Donn Byrne. *New York Herald Tribune*, June 24, 1928.
Sunday magazine feature article, containing a number of interesting and amusing anecdotes concerning Donn Byrne, but with little factual biographical or bibliographical information.

14. McCardell, Roy L. Donn Byrne, poet, philologist, author of romantic novels of dithyrambic diction. *New York Morning Telegraph*, April 22, 1923.
Same comment as under "13," above.

15. Leslie, Shane. A literary beau sabreur. *Outlook*, London, 61:781–782, June 23, 1928.
Eulogistic critique of Donn Byrne's literary career.

16. Fox, Paul Hervey. Donn Byrne, himself. *Saturday evening post*, 190.10, p. 27, 117, September 8, 1917.
Facetious sketch of Donn Byrne at an early stage in his writing career.

17. Devlin, Joseph. Donn Byrne and his new book. *National magazine*, Boston, 56:9, p. 398–399, 422, May, 1928.
A review of *Crusade*, but contains in addition a great deal of miscellaneous information concerning its author.

18. Edelman, Katherine. Donn Byrne, novelist and short story writer. *Kansas City, Mo., Star*, June 30, 1928.

19. Johnson, Merle. American first editions. New York: Bowker, 1942. (Fourth ed., revised by Jacob Blanck.)

Pages 84–86 contain the established data concerning identification of the Byrne first editions.

20. Kunitz, Stanley J. Authors to-day and yesterday. New York: Wilson, 1933, p. 121–124.

Excellent brief summary of Donn Byrne's life and literary achievements, with a short bibliography. See also, by same author in collaboration with H. Haycraft (20a), Twentieth century authors. New York: Wilson, 1942, p. 232–233.

21. Marble, Anne Russell. A study of the modern novel. New York: Appleton, 1930, p. 64–67.

Same comment as under "20," above.

22. Baker, Ernest A. History of the English novel. London: Witherby.

Vol. 9 (1938), p. 335, brief mention, vol. 10 (1939), p. 196–198, critical review of Donn Byrne's work.

23. Dictionary of American biography: Brian Oswald Donn Byrne.

Short article by Mr. Frank Monaghan, mainly biographical, with a few bibliographical references.

24. Newspaper interviews, on the occasion of Donn Byrne's visit to America in 1925: *a. New York Evening Post,* June 11, 1925, p. 14; *b. New York Sun,* June 17, 1925, p. 36; *c. New York Telegram-Mail,* June 24, 1925; *d. New York Times,* June 10, 1925. Quite possibly other New York journals also ran similar material; files of the *Herald, Tribune, Globe, World, Telegraph, News, Mirror, Graphic,* etc., and the Brooklyn papers have not been examined.

25. Two typescript pages of biographical notes, prepared at Riverside around 1920 by Miss Davids under Donn Byrne's direction. A copy is in the Wetherbee Collection. References to these notes will be found under "Miscellaneous Writings," *Poems,* and *The Foolish matrons.*

26. Keller, Mary E. A critical study of the life and novels of Donn Byrne. Master's thesis submitted to the Department of English, April 23, 1948, University of Southern California, Los Angeles.

B. *Mention of Donn Byrne in Various Standard Reference Books.*

Note: In the majority of references cited below, there is only very brief mention of Donn Byrne; in many instances, the articles contain gross inaccuracies, mainly, these references are listed more for the sake of completeness than because they add anything to our knowledge of the subject. Items of more than passing interest are marked with an asterisk.

40. New international yearbook; New York: Dodd, Mead, 1923–28.

41. Discher, L. A., and I. Halpern. American first editions. *Publishers' weekly,* 117:337, January 18, 1930.

GENERAL REFERENCE LIST

42. Baker and Packman. Guide to the best fiction. New York: Macmillan, 1932, p. 84.

43. Edgar, Pelham. Art of the novel. New York: Macmillan, 1933, p. 352.

44. Blankenship, R. American literature. New York: Holt, 1931, p. 698–699.

45. Hatcher, H. Creating the modern American novel. New York: Farrar & Rinehart, 1935, p. 211.

46. Weygandt, C. A century of the English novel. New York: Century, 1928, p. 38.

47. Hansen, A. C. Twentieth century forces in European fiction. Chicago: ALA Press, 1934, p. 113.

48. The Columbia encyclopedia (1935).

49. Drury, F. K. W., and W. E. Simnet. What books shall I read? Boston: Houghton Mifflin, 1933, p. 245.

50. Nield, J. Guide to historical fiction. London: Mathews and Marrot, 1929, p. 9, 38, 143f.

51. Overton, Grant. One hour of the American novel. Philadelphia: Lippincott, 1929, p. 139.

52. Van Doren, Carl. Contemporary American novelists, 1900–20. New York: Macmillan, 1931, p. 176. See also, "95," below.

53. Drew, E. A. The modern novel. New York: Harcourt, Brace, 1926, p. 252.

54. Jessup, A. Representative American short stories. New York: Allyn & Bacon, 1923, p. 62.

55. Sullivan, Mark. Our times. The Twenties. New York: Scribner's.

56. MacMinn, G. R., and H. Eagleson. College readings in the modern short story. New York: Ginn, 1931.

57. One thousand books for the senior high school library. Chicago: ALA, 1935, p. 60.

58. Standard catalogue for high school libraries. New York: Wilson, 1928.

59. Who was who, 1916–1928. London: A. & C. Black.

60. New Standard encyclopedia, F. H. Vizetelly, editor. New York: Funk & Wagnalls, 1934. Vol. 4, p. 484.

61. Hartwick, Harry. The foreground of American fiction. New York: American Book Co., 1934, p. 187.

62. Manly, J. M., and E. Rickert. Contemporary American literature. New York: Harcourt, Brace, 1929, p. 31.

DONN BYRNE BIBLIOGRAPHY

63. Dickinson, Asa Don. Best books of our time, 1901–1925. New York: Doubleday, Doran, 1928, p. 51. See also his (63a) *Best books of the decade 1926–35*. New York: Wilson, 1937, p. 37.

64. Graham, Bessie. The bookman's manual. New York: Bowker, 1935, p. 533–534, 670; 1941, p. 614, 773.

65. Johnson, Merle. High spots of American literature. New York: Bowker, 1929.

66. Kunitz, S. J., and H. Haycroft. Junior book of authors. New York: Wilson, 1934, p. 74.

*67. Baker, Harry T. Contemporary short story. New York: Heath, 1916, p. 22–24, 114, 129, 193, 215, 230, 261.

68. Bulletin of the Public Library of the City of Boston. Fourth series, vols. 2, 4, 5 et seq.

69. Logasa, H. Historical fiction. Philadelphia: McKinley, 1934, p. 25, 34.

70. Thrall, W. F., and A. Hibbard. Handbook to literature. New York: Doubleday, Doran, 1936. p. 578.

71. Standard catalog (Fiction list). New York: Wilson, 1923, 1931, 1934.

72. Targ, William. American first editions and their prices. Chicago: Black Archer Press, 1931, p. 16.

*73. Hefling, H., and J. W. Dyde. Index to contemporary biography and criticism. Boston: Faxon, 1934, p. 60.

*74. Book review digest (annual volumes). New York: Wilson.

75. New concise pictorial encyclopedia, Nella Braddy, ed. New York: Garden City, 1938, p. 176.

*76. Who's who. London: A. and C. Black, vols. for 1927 and 1928.

*77. Who's who in America. Chicago: A. N. Marquis & Co., vols. 1916–1929.

78. New American encyclopedia. New York: Books, Inc., 1938.

79. Who's who among North American authors. Los Angeles: Golden Syndicate Pub. Co., 1927–29, p. 145.

80. Good reading, ed. by A. H. Townsend. Chicago: National Council of Teachers of English, 1938, p. 62.

81. National cyclopedia of American biography. New York: White, 1932; vol. 22, p. 295. See also (81a) *White's Conspectus of American biography*. New York: White, 1937, 2nd ed., p. 314.

82. Williams, Blanche C. Handbook on story writing. New York: Dodd, Mead, 1918. See also, by same author: (82a) *How to study "The best short stories."* New York: Small, Maynard, 1919, p. v, 42–43.

GENERAL REFERENCE LIST

83. American year book. New York, 1915 et seq. See vols. for 1925, 1926, and 1927.

84. The World almanac. New York. Annual. Only mention of Donn Byrne is in 1923 volume, p. 135.

85. Halleck, Reuben P. Romance of American literature. New York: American Book Co., 1934, p. 378.

86. Nethercott, A. H. A book of long stories. New York: Macmillan, 1927, p. 716.

87. Roos, Jean C. What shall we read next? New York: Wilson, 1935.

88. Gold star list of American fiction. Syracuse: Syracuse Public Library, annual vols.

89. Hartford reading list. New York: Holt, annual vols.

90. Van Nostrand, J. Subject index to high school fiction. Chicago: ALA, 1938.

91. Mahoney, B. E., and E. Whitney. Realm of gold in children's books. New York: Doubleday, Doran, 1929, p. 664.

92. American Library Association catalogues. Brief mention in volumes for 1912–1921, 1926, 1926–31.

93. Catalogue of the London Library. Supplement, 1920–1928, p. 167.

94. Lenrow, E. Reader's guide to prose fiction. New York: Appleton-Century, 1940, p. 78, 84, 85.

95. Van Doren, Carl. The American novel, 1789–1939. New York: Macmillan, 1940, p. 323.

96. Hart, J. D. Oxford companion to American literature. New York: Oxford, 1941, p. 200.

97. Burke, W. J., and W. D. Howe. American authors and books. New York: Gramercy Pub. Co., 1943, p. 111.

98. Webster's biographical dictionary. Springfield, Mass.: Merriam, 1943, p. 429.

99. Preston, Wheeler. American biographies. New York: Harper, 1940, p. 139.

100. Ricker, P. M. An analytical bibliography of universal collected biography. London: Library Association, 1934.

101. Catalogue of novels and tales by Catholic writers. Dublin: Dublin Central Catholic Library Association, 1928.

102. Guide to Catholic literature, 1888–1940. Detroit, 1940, p. 154.

DONN BYRNE BIBLIOGRAPHY

C. Donn Byrne Items in Various Booksellers' Catalogues and Auction Records.

Note. No attempt has been made to make the following list complete; there are listed only items of unusual interest or rarity, such as manuscripts, presentation copies, or other association material.

151. American Art Association — Anderson Galleries, New York City:

  a. Catalogue no. 4104, sale April 18–19, 1934. Item 145, manuscript, MMP.
  b. Catalogue no. 4296, sale January 28–29, 1937. Item 61, manuscript, BR.
  c. Catalogue no. 4320, sale April 14–15, 1937. Item 42b, manuscript, WB.
  d. Catalogue no. 4346, sale November 11–12, 1937. Items 50–52, manuscripts, O'M, FoH and PoB.
  e. Catalogue no. 4201, sale November 13, 1935. Inscribed presentation copies, MMP and SwW.
  f. Catalogue no. 4228, sale January 29–30, 1936. 1st ed., with d. j., MMP.
  g. Catalogue no. 4175, sale April 24–25, 1935. 1st ed., with d. j., MMP.
  h. Catalogue no. 4253, sale April 22–23, 1936. Inscribed presentation copy, SB.
  i. Catalogue no. 4201, sale November 13, 14, 1935. Inscribed presentation copies, SwW and MMP.

152. Parke-Bernet Galleries, New York City:

  a. Catalogue 11, February 25, 1938. Manuscripts of SB, FM and I.
  b. Catalogue 13, March 3, 1938. Inscribed presentation copies, SB, BS.
  c. Catalogue 66, November 21–22, 1938. 1st ed., with d. j., SwW.
  d. Catalogue 140, November 15–16, 1939. Inscribed presentation copy, SwW. 1st ed., with d. j., MMP (the ALS attributed to Donn Byrne, described as part of this item, was not in fact written by him).
  e. Catalogue, January 23, 24, 1945. Inscribed presentation copies, SwW and MMP.

153. Argosy Book Stores, New York City:

  a. Catalogue no. 117. Inscribed presentation copy, FM.
  b. Catalogue no. 187, August, 1941. 1st ed., with d. j., SwW.

154. Retz and Storm, Inc., New York City:

  a. Catalogue no. six, 1938. Manuscript, GG (POB).

155. Argus Book Shop, Chicago:

  a. Along the North Wall — Section Six (1937). Inscribed presentation copy, SwW.

156. Chaucer Head Book Shop, New York City:

  a. Fifteenth anniversary catalogue. Inscribed presentation copy, MMP. 1st ed., SwW, with review clippings tipped in; this described as probably Donn Byrne's own copy.

[74]

GENERAL REFERENCE LIST

157. Chiswick Book Shop, New York City:
a. Catalogue, October, 1945. Inscribed presentation copy, FM.

158. Hoosier Bookshop, Indianapolis:
a. Catalogue no. 80, 1940. Manuscripts, BS and Cr.

159. Scribner Book Store, New York City:
a. Catalogue no. 122. Inscribed presentation copy, SwW; another copy, same title, in original d. w., but not inscribed.

160. Howard S. Mott, Jr., New York City:
a. Catalogue no. 9 (1939). 1st ed., with d. j , MMP.
b. Catalogue no. 14. 1st ed., with d. j., SB.

161. Ritter-Hopson Galleries, Inc., Newark:
a. Catalogue no. 6, November 11, 1930. 1st ed., HH, with ALS of Donn Byrne tipped in.

D. Obituary Articles.

Note· The following list has deliberately been made fairly extensive, perhaps disproportionately so. This has been done, first, to give some idea of the general interest in Donn Byrne at the time of his death, and, second, because many of the writers of these articles took the occasion to sum up his life and works, and to evaluate his literary career. The references marked with asterisks have particular individual interest.

* 176. Time, 12:1, p. 25, July 2, 1928.

177. London mercury, 18:236, July, 1928.

178. Boston Herald, June 20, 1928.

179. Baltimore Sun, June 20, 1928.

180. New York World, June 20, 1928. See also, * (180a) New York World, June 22, 1928; Harry Hansen, "The First reader."

* 181. Outlook, New York, 149:367, July 4, 1928.

* 182. Brickell, Herschel: North American review, 226:846, August, 1928.

* 183. Bookman, London, 74:211, July, 1928.

* 184. New York World, June 21, 1928. Letter, Shane Conway.

* 185. Chicago Tribune, August 4, 1928. London letter, Frank Swinnerton.

* 186. T. P. O'Connor: T. P.'s weekly, July 28, 1928.

* 187. Louisville Herald Post, June 24, 1928.

* 188. Times, London, 21d, 11d; June 20, 1928.

DONN BYRNE BIBLIOGRAPHY

* 189. New York Times, June 20, 1928.
The AP account, which appeared in most metropolitan dailies on this date. See also New York Herald Tribune, Boston Evening Transcript, Chicago Tribune, etc.

190. San Francisco Argonaut, June 23, 1928. See also, *ibid.*, (190a) June 30, 1928.

191. Philadelphia Public Ledger, 14:4, June 23, 1928.

192. Pittsburgh Post Gazette, June 14, 1928 (contains the poem of David S. Wilkins).

193. San Francisco Chronicle, June 24, 1928, p. 10D.

194. San Francisco Bulletin, July 25, 1928.

195. Atlanta Constitution, June 20, 1928.

196. Marry, Peter: "Donn Byrne. In memoriam." Eulogy, stated to have appeared in the *Publishers' weekly*, date not determined.

197. Publishers' weekly, 113:25, p. 2545, June 23, 1928. See also, *ibid.*, (197a) p. 2541.

198. Publishers' circular, 128.3234, p. 843, June 23, 1928.

* 199. Glasgow Evening Times, June 20, 1928.

* 200. Washington, D. C., Star, July 4, 1928. Obituary quotes others appearing in the following newspapers: Regina Leader, South Bend Tribune, Oakland Tribune, Dubuque American Tribune, Hartford Courant, Norfolk Ledger Dispatch, Louisville Times, Madison State Journal, Oklahoma Daily Oklahoman, Buffalo News, Pasadena Herald, Kansas City Post, Canton Daily News, Philadelphia Record, Port Arthur News, Passaic Herald.

* 201. Dublin Sunday Mail, July 2, 1928.

202. Glasgow Evening News, June 20, 1928.

203. Inverness Courier, July 10, 1928.

* 204. Cork Examiner, June 20, 1928. (With photographs of scene of fatal accident.) See also, *ibid.*, June 29, 1928.

* 205. Dublin Sunday Independent, July 8, 1928.

206. Manchester Dispatch, June 20, 1928.

207. Liverpool Post, June 23, 1928.

* 208. London Daily Mail, June 20, 1928.

209. Irish News, June 20, 1928.

* 210. Irish Times, June 20, 1928; June 28, 1928; July 7, 1928; June 21, 1928.

211. The Newsagent, June 30, 1928.

GENERAL REFERENCE LIST

212. Manchester Guardian, June 22, 1928.
213. Belfast Weekly News, June 28, 1928.
214. Rugby Observer, June 23, 1928.
215. London Daily Observer, June 20, 1928.
216. London Daily Express, June 20, 1928; June 22, 1928.
217. New York Sun, June 20, 1928.
218. Gloucester Citizen, June 19, 1928.
219. London Graphic, June 30, 1928.
220. London Morning Post, June 20, 1928.
221. Aberdeen Evening Express, June 21, 1928.
222. Chatham Evening Chronicle, June 20, 1928.
223. Burton Evening Gazette, June 20, 1928.
224. Nashville Banner, July 1, 1928.
* 225. Spokane Spokesman Review, June 21, 1928.
* 226. Los Angeles Times, June 23, 1928.
227. Book review digest, June, 1928.
228. Philadelphia Bulletin, June 20, 1928.
229. Hartford Times, June 20, 1928.
230. Syracuse Herald, June 20, 1928.
231. Denver News, June 20, 1928.
232. Wilkes Barre News, June 26, 1928.
233. Providence Journal, June 24, 1928.
234. Saturday review of literature, June 30, 1928.
235. St. Louis Star, June 19, 1928.
236. Salt Lake City Deseret News, June 30, 1928.
237. Springfield Republican, June 20, 1928.
238. Nashville Banner, June 24, 1928.
* 239. New York Telegram, June 21, 1928. See also June 19, 1928.
240. Minneapolis Journal, July 1, 1928.
241. Portland Oregonian, June 20, 1928.
242. Variety, June 27, 1928.

* 213. Passaic News, June 22, 1928.
214. Springfield Union, June 21, 1928.
245. Atlanta Journal June 26, 1928.
246. Indianapolis Star, June 29, 1928.
247. St. Louis Times, June 21, 1928.
* 248. The Tablet, Brooklyn, N. Y., "Managing editor's column," June 23, 1928.
* 249. Canadian bookman, October, 1928, p. 292. Poem, "To Donn Byrne," by C F. Lloyd.
* 250. T. P.'s weekly, 10.245, p. 331, July 7, 1928.
251. San Francisco Call, June 21, 1928.
252. Chicago Tribune, June 22, 1928; July 2, 1928.
253. Louisville Times, June 21, 1928.
254. Kansas City Journal, June 21, 1928.
255. St. Louis Post Dispatch, June 20, 1928.
256. New Orleans Times Picayune, June 22, 1928.
257. St. Paul Dispatch, June 21, 1928.
258. Detroit Free Press, June 22, 1928.
259. Des Moines Register, June 21, 1928.
260. Washington Post, June 24, 1928.
261. Montreal Star, June 20, 1928.
262. Akron Beacon Journal, June 20, 1928.
263. Philadelphia News, June 20, 1928.
264. Buffalo News, June 20, 1928.
265. Brooklyn Standard Union, June 20, 1928.
266. New York Herald Tribune, June 21, 1928.
* 267. Bronx, New York, Home News, July 1, 1928.
268. Baltimore Observer, June 23, 1928.
* 269. Boston Traveler, June 21, 1928.
* 270. Montgomery Advertiser, June 20, 1928.
271. Louisville Herald Post, June 24, 1928.
272. Peoria Transcript, June 20, 1928.
273. Irish World, June 30, 1928.

GENERAL REFERENCE LIST

E. Miscellaneous References, Chiefly of Minor Interest.

301. Short history of the Saturday Evening Post. Philadelphia: Curtis Publishing Co., 1936, p. 22, 32.

302. Reviews of Mr. Macauley's biography: *Bookman*, London, 77:341, March, 1930; *Boston Herald*, December 7, 1929; *Times literary supplement*, London, 29:162, February 27, 1930; *Review of reviews*, New York, 80:6, p. 19, December, 1929; *Saturday review of literature*, 6:717, February 8, 1930 (James T. Farrell); *Spectator*, 144:437, March 15, 1930; *A. L. A. Booklist*, 26:201, February, 1930; *Bookman*, New York, 70:6, p. vi, February, 1930; * *New York Herald Tribune books*, December 1, 1929, p. 18 (Shaemus O'Sheel); *Churchman*, 140:24, p. 15, December 14, 1929; *Cleveland Open shelf*, December, 1929, p. 154; *New York Evening Post*, December 7, 1929, p. 9M (Edwin Seaver); *New York Times*, February 9, 1930, p. 19, *Pittsburgh monthly bulletin*, 35:10, February, 1930, *Pratt Institute quarterly*, Spring, 1930, p. 36; *Wisconsin library bulletin*, 26:67, February, 1930; *Publishers' circular*, 132:3322, p. 307, March 1, 1930; * *Catholic news*, October 25, 1930, p. 10 (Terence O'Hanlon); *America*, 42:15, p. 366, January 18, 1930, *English journal*, 19:1, p. 90, January, 1930.

303. Abdullah, Achmed. The cat had nine lives. New York: Farrar & Rinehart, 1933, p. 37. See also, by same author: (303a) Deliver us from evil. New York: Putnam, 1939.

304. Topeka Capitol, November 3, 1929. American or Irish?

305. Saturday review of literature, 6:45, p. 1100, May 31, 1930.

306. Bookman, New York. "The Gossip shop" column, 51:1, p. 126, March, 1920; 51:2, p. 253, April, 1920; 53:6, p. 570, August, 1921; 54:2, p. 185–186, October, 1921; 60:3, p. 380, November, 1924; 61:6, p. 729, August, 1925.

307. New York Times, news items, in addition to references cited elsewhere: March 2, 1922, 21:1; July 1, 1922, 3:8; June 10, 1925, 14:2; June 22, 1928, 25:5; November 8, 1928 (Burton lecture); May 28, 1929, 34:3; November 11, 1929, 19:3.

308. Saturday review of literature, 15: sup. 13, 18, March 27, 1937.

309. Slocombe, George. The tumult and the shouting. New York: Macmillan, 1936, p. 222.

310. Century magazine. "Among our contributors" column, 102:4, adv., August, 1921; 102:5, adv., September, 1921; 102:6, adv., October, 1921; 104:2, adv., June, 1922; 104:3, adv., July, 1922; 104:4, adv., August, 1922; 104:5, adv., September, 1922; 109:2, adv., December, 1924.

311. O. Henry Memorial Award prize stories. New York: Doubleday, Doran. Annual.
See notes under the following short stories: Bargain price, Reynardine, Keeper of the bridge, Wisdom buildeth her house, Story against women, Wall that is high, Rivers of Damascus, Green eyes.

DONN BYRNE BIBLIOGRAPHY

312. Published photographs, drawings, and sketches of Donn Byrne. (List is believed to be quite complete; most, if not all, of the apparent omissions will be found to be duplications of one or another of the portraits mentioned.)

   a. Macauley, Thurston. Donn Byrne, bard of Armagh. Both the American and English editions contain several excellent photographs, and each contains one or more not included in the other.
   b. Bookman, London, supplement, 73:32a, October, 1927. The H. M. G. Wilson crayon portrait.
   c. Collier's magazine, 71:5, p. 30, February 3, 1923. Early photograph.
   d. Time, 9:37, April 25, 1927.
   e. Bookman, New York, 54:2, October, 1921. Sketch.
   f. New York Herald Tribune books, June 30, 1929, p. 7. Drawing by Edwin Earle.
   g. Red book, 29:6, contents page, October, 1917.
   h. ibid., 30:5, p. 4, March, 1918.
   i. Saturday evening post, 190:10, p. 27, September 8, 1917.
   j. Century magazine, 103:6, adv., April, 1922. The George Bellows drawing.
   k. Hearst's international, 39:1, p. 2, January, 1921. Early photograph.
   l. Century magazine, 102:6, adv., October, 1921.
   m. Bookman, London, 69:413, p. 258, February, 1926.
   n. New York Herald Tribune books, June 24, 1928. Drawing by Beatrice Beard.
   o. Century magazine, 105:2, adv., December, 1922.
   p. Malone, Andrew E. Donn Byrne, an Irish realist. Contains several excellent photographs.
   q. Bookman, London, 76:131, May, 1929. The E. Brooks Hughes photograph.
   r. Milwaukee Journal, March 31, 1928. Caricature.
   s. Century magazine, 109:2, adv., December, 1924. Photograph by H. G. Oakley.
   t. Adcock, A. St. John. Gods of modern Grub Street. First publication of the E. O. Hoppé photograph.
   u. New York Tribune, October 31, 1920.
   v. San Francisco Chronicle, March 22, 1925. The Bastian drawing.
   w. T. P.'s weekly, 4:104, p. 811, October 17, 1925.
   x. Harper's magazine, 141:845, adv., October, 1920.
   y. Time, 7:20, p. 37, May 17, 1926.
   z. Kansas City, Mo., Star, March 31, 1928. Drawing, by Roy Gray, after photograph.
   aa. Milwaukee Journal, April 14, 1928. Caricature by Russell Henderson.

313. Golden book magazine, 15:85, p. 4a, January, 1932. See also, *ibid.*, 15:87, p. 288, March, 1932.

314. Wilson's bulletin, New York, 6:36, September, 1931.

315. The World of books. Scripps College, Claremont, Cal., ? date. p. 40.

GENERAL REFERENCE LIST

316. Haines, H. E. Living with books. New York: Columbia University Press, 1935, p. 458.

317. Lucas, E. F. Reading, writing and remembering. New York: Harper's, 1932, p. 18.

318. Des Moines Sunday Register, April 15, 1928. Portrait, "Who is Donn Byrne?"

319. Boston Evening Transcript, February 12, 1938, IV, 2:4. "The Librarian."

320. American book-prices current. New York: Bowker. Annual.
No mention of Byrne books until 1928; in this and subsequent years through 1945, various books and manuscripts are listed, together with their auction prices.

321. The Best short stories, edited by Edward J. O'Brien. New York: Dodd, Mead. Annual.
Only Donn Byrne story to be reprinted in any of these volumes was "The wake," which appeared in the 1915 edition. Mention and citation of various of the other short stories occurs in the volumes from 1916 to 1935 inclusive, and in that for 1937. Details are given, in this compilation, in connection with the individual stories.

322. The Best British short stories, edited by Edward J. O'Brien. New York: Dodd, Mead. Annual.
Mention of Donn Byrne in volumes 1925–1927, and 1929–34. In most instances, various references are cited to reviews and other articles.

323. New York Times, March 6, 1925, 10:2.
Account of the WNBA dinner, at which were distributed the presentation copies of *O'Malley of Shanganagh*.

324. Bolton, Theodore. American book illustrators. New York: Bowker, 1938, p. 14, 53.

325. Lynd, Robert. Irish and English. London: Griffiths, ? date.
This book, now out of print, is the one referred to by Mr. Macauley (p. 11, Century ed.) describing Donn Byrne as a young boy.

326. Publishers' weekly, 133:1937, May 14, 1938.

327. Saturday evening post, 211:8, p. 51, August 20, 1938.

328. Reviews of Dr. Wetherbee's preliminary bibliography (Gen. Ref. List, no. 4): *Publishers' weekly*, 133:17, p. 1696, April 23, 1928; *ibid.*, 134:8, p. 524, August 20, 1938; *Baltimore Evening Sun*, February 19, 1938.

329. Golden book magazine, 19:112, p. 4a, April, 1934.

330. Everybody's magazine, 54:3, p. 117, March, 1926.

331. Scribner's magazine, 72:2, p. 13, adv., August, 1922.

332. Ross, Ishbell. Geography, Inc. *Scribner's magazine*, 103:6, p. 23–27, 57, June, 1938.

DONN BYRNE BIBLIOGRAPHY

333. Ellis, Jessie Croft. General index to illustrations Boston: Faxon, 1931.

334. Saturday review of literature, 11:7, p. 79, September 1, 1934.
Review, by R. H. Macdougall, of Thomas Lennon's *The Laughing journey*, with some discussion of his and Donn Byrne's literary style.

335. Weston, B. E., and A. C. Frasca, ed. Holden's Private book collectors. New York: Bowker, 1936, p. 131.

336. Braithwaite, W. S. B., ed. Anthology of magazine verse. Cambridge, etc. Annual.
Poems by Donn Byrne are mentioned in volumes for 1913, 1914, and 1916.

337. San Francisco Chronicle, February 1, 1931, 4D:7.
"The Bibliophile." Article about Donn Byrne, with brief bibliography.

338. New York Times book review, August 14, 1938, p. 8.
Brief mention in article on Irish literature by Sean O'Faolain.

339. Atlanta Constitution, October 9, 1921, 1F:1. See also March 15, 1925, 4:3.

340. Book prices current. London: Witherby. Annual.
Mention of Donn Byrne books in volumes for 1933, 1936, 1940, 1941.

341. Book auction records. London: Stevens. Annual.
Mention of Donn Byrne books in volumes for 1936, 1939, 1940, and 1944. The 1939 volume mentions a copy of MMP with an inserted ALS.

342. Hearst's international, 34:1, editorial page, July, 1918.

343. *ibid.*, 37:3, editorial page, March, 1920.

344. Van Patten, Nathan. Index to bibliographies, 1923–32. Stanford University Press, 1934, p. 38.

345. T. P.'s and Cassell's weekly:

a. 3:77, p. 926, April 11, 1925. "How Donn Byrne became an author."

b. 8:194, p. 382, July 15, 1927. Mr. Robert Keable lists MMP as one of his six favorite novels.

c. 9:221, p. 457, January 21, 1928. Obituary, Mr. Keable mentioning the fact that in his library of 2000 volumes, there were but six novels, one of which was MMP.

346. New York World, May 19, 1926, p. 15.
Mention of Donn Byrne, and of HH, in Mr. Heywood Broun's column, "It seems to me." See also, *ibid.*, May 12, 1926, p. 17.

347. Century magazine, 105:1, p. 26, November, 1922. "Youth grows up," by Samson Raphaelson.

348. Frank, Glenn. Brief mention of Donn Byrne in following articles for McClure Newspaper Syndicate: *a.* Politics and salmon, June 21, 1929; *b.* Politics

GENERAL REFERENCE LIST

and steel, June 22, 1929; *c.* Politics holds the key, January 16, 1933; *d.* Getting educated politically, December 20, 1934.

349. Catholic news, October 25, 1930, p. 10.
"Was Donn Byrne a Catholic?" Reprinted from Terence O'Hanlon, in *The Father Mathew record*, Dublin.

350. Parrington, Vernon L. The beginnings of critical realism in America. New York: Harcourt, Brace, 1930, p. 377–378.

351. Driver, H. B. Bostonian's literary pilgrimage to Castle of Donn-Byrne. *Boston Sunday Globe*, October 8, 1933.

352. Most of the reviews of books by Maurice Walsh compare the writing of this author with that of Donn Byrne; this is partly due to the fact that Mr. Walsh's publishers frequently refer to him in their "blurbs" as "the literary successor of Donn Byrne." No attempt has been made to list even a fraction of the instances in which this comparison occurs, but the following half-dozen or so are given as typical examples:

a. Boston Herald, January 28, 1939. Review of *Sons of the swordmaker.*

b. New York Times book review, January 8, 1939, p. 6. Same.

c. Chicago Tribune, July 14, 1934, p. 6. Review of *The Road to nowhere.*

d. New York Herald Tribune, July 9, 1934, p. 7. Same.

e. New York Herald Tribune books, July 8, 1934, p. 7. Same.

f. Boston Herald, February 19, 1938, 6:5. Review of *The Dark rose.*

g. New York Times book review, February 27, 1938, p. 7. Same.

353. Time, 33:18, p. 49–50, May 1, 1939. "U. S. illustrators." Mention of Donn Byrne and of many of the artists who illustrated his magazine stories.

354. Publishers' weekly, 109:20, p. 1609, May 15, 1926. News item concerning current demand for first editions, with mention of Donn Byrne.

355. Bulletin of the Poetry Society of America. Mention of poems by Donn Byrne in issues of January, March, and April, 1914; November, 1915; May, 1916.

356. Stuart, Sheila. Another sonnet. Chicago Tribune, "A line o' type or two" column, 1928. Poem mentioning Donn Byrne.

357. Morgan, Vera A. Vocations in short stories. Chicago: A. L. A., 1938. Lists WB and AoFS as "books which yielded no vocational material."

358. Thompson, Charles Willis. The real Joyce Kilmer. *Catholic world*, 149:892, p. 423–429, July, 1939.
Contains several anecdotes concerning Donn Byrne and Joyce Kilmer. See also, by same author: (358a) Another side of Kilmer. *Columbia*, 4:12, p. 33, 47, July, 1925.

* 359. The Recorder (New York: American Irish Historical Society). 10:1, p. 11–13, January 2, 1939. "Donn Byrne." Biographical sketch.

360. McQuilland, Louis J. Literary Ireland of today. *Book notes*, Hartford, Conn., 5:5, p. 247-250, August - September, 1927.

361. Requests for information or assistance in connection with Donn Byrne research, or for material in connection with Donn Byrne collecting: *a. New York Times book review*, November 19, 1939, p. 12; *b. New York World Telegram*, November 22, 1933, Personals column, p. 38, 1. 7, *c. Times*, London, August 18, 1944, Personal column; *d. Saturday review*, September 21, 1946, Personals column; *e. Publishers' weekly*, 133:17, p. 1696, April 23, 1938; *f. Publishers' weekly*, 137:21, p 2094, May 25, 1940; *g. Publishers' weekly*, 138:11, p. 962, September 14, 1940.

362. New York Herald Tribune books. ix:13, 1, August 18, 1940

363. Rivoallan, A. Littérature irlandaise contemporaine. Paris: Hachette, 1939, p. 147-148.

364. Preston, Wheeler. American biographies. New York: Harper, 1940, p. 139.

365. Annual report. The Houghton Library, 1944. Cambridge, Mass., p. 30; *ibid.*, 1945-46, p. 35.

366. The blue guides: Ireland. Findlay Muirhead, ed. London: Benn, 1932, p. li.

367. Tourist map of Ireland. Dublin: Irish Tourist Association, no date.

368. New York Herald, June 24, 1923. Hugh Walpole.

369. British weekly, September 27, 1923. News item.

370. Publishers' weekly, August 24, 1929.
Description of library of Byrd Polar Expedition, with comment "the most widely read author has been Donn Byrne."

371. South Bend Tribune, April 11, 1935.
O. O. McIntyre writes about Charleston, S. C., and comments, "the late Donn Byrne thought it the most romantically beautiful city in America."

372. Cross, Ethan Allen. A book of the short story. New York: American Book Co., 1934.
Contains mention of Donn Byrne.

373. McCloskey, John P. Modern English composition.
Contains selections, with comments, from writings of modern authors, including Donn Byrne.

Appendix

Note 1

Elsewhere in this book, listed under the individual titles, mention has been made of various inscribed presentation copies of Donn Byrne's works. Some of the inscriptions are given below:

SwW

In revenge for having enticed me to read Zarathustra and Gorky and on condition that it is not used to blackmail me in my honorable and inartistic old age; this for Carl Gauss, Sincerely from Donn Byrne.

To Mr. & Mrs. E. J. Fay (not forgetting Mr. Barton), from the author, Donn Byrne, Xmas, 1915.

To my old companion man-at-arms, Joyce Kilmer, in admiration and friendship, Donn Byrne, New York, Nov. 16th, 1915.

To J. A. McCann, with appreciation for the encouragement in the dark days. Donn Byrne, February 19, 1916.

Mon ami Metts, "much obliged to meet you!" Donn Byrne. May 27, 1916.

SB

To Tom Walsh, in admiration and friendship, Donn Byrne, Xmas, 1919.

FM

To Arnold Daly with the cordial friendship and sincere appreciation of Donn Byrne, Noel, 1920.

MMP

To Amy Lowell, reverently, Donn Byrne. November, 1921.

To Sewell Haggard, Never forgetting that his advice, support, and encouragement made my best writing possible. Very sincerely, Donn Byrne. October 10, 1921.

To S. Jay Kaufman, in memory of another Irish tale, "General John Regan" — old ghostlike days! Cordially, Donn Byrne, October 31, 1921.

To James L. Ford, in grateful remembrance for a review of "The Strangers' Banquet" when the author was very discouraged. Donn Byrne, November, 1921.

To Lovell M. Palmer, Jr., supporting Dan Parker's contention that he is a gentleman, a sportsman and a scholar! Sincerely, Donn Byrne, November, 1921.

BS

Do mo caraid, Sean Leslie, O Brian na Beirne-donn, "Donn Byrne."

Note 2

Out of many bibliographical questions to which the present compilation does not provide answers, the following have been selected as being of possible interest for further study:

a. The periodical and date of publication of the magazine appearance of the short story "Hail and farewell."

DONN BYRNE BIBLIOGRAPHY

b. Periodicals, and publication dates, of the poems "The king of Ireland's daughter" and "The poet reproves."

c. Original publication of the poem about the San Francisco earthquake, mentioned by Malone and others; date of its re-printing in *The United Irishman*.

d. The newspaper appearance of Donn Byrne's letter concerning *Hangman's House* (see Macauley, p. 118, etc.); the journals (and dates) containing the articles referred to in the letter.

e. Identification of editorials written by Donn Byrne for the *New York Globe*, and possibly for other newspapers.

f. Details concerning translations of the books into foreign languages (see under "Translations").

g. Data concerning Donn Byrne's early lectures for the Brooklyn Board of Education (see Mr. Greenberg's thesis).

h. Data concerning the motion pictures mentioned under "Cinematizations," and concerning other of the stories that may have been made into screen productions.

i. Possible writing by Donn Byrne for one or more of the "little magazines" published in New York and elsewhere during the 1912–1922 period (e. g., *Bruno's weekly*, the *Broadway magazine*, etc.).

j. Details concerning the publication or possible production of the playlet, "Down by the tan-yard side." See under Miscellaneous Writings.

k. Files of the following magazines have not been consulted for the periods indicated. Possibly additional Byrne material may be found in some of them: *McClure's* — prior to 1913, subsequent to 1915; *McLean's* — all issues, *Snappy stories* — 1915, 1917; *Leslie's* — all issues; *Pearson's* — all issues; *People's* — all issues, all English and Irish magazines and newspapers.

l. Identification of specific articles written for the *New Standard dictionary*, possibly the *Catholic encyclopedia*, and possibly one or two other standard reference books.

m. Mention of Donn Byrne by various New York "colyumnists" during the early New York period. F. P. A., S. Jay Kaufman, Frank Sullivan, among others, have been stated to have mentioned him at various times in their columns, but definite details have not been discovered. Probable mention also in *New York Times magazine* while under editorship of Joyce Kilmer (ca. 1913–1917).

n. Details concerning Professor Richard Burton's lecture on Donn Byrne, given at Columbia, November 7, 1928.

Note 3. Variants of the Name "Donn Byrne."

If the writer we know as Donn Byrne had ever been able to obtain a birth certificate, which for some unexplained reason he never could, his name would not have appeared there thus, but as "Bernard Byrne." This is attested by the Baptismal Register of the Church of the Guardian Angels, New York. The date of baptism is given as December 1, 1889. During the next fifteen years or so, during his childhood in Armagh, he was more commonly known by the Irish equivalent of this name, or Brian O'Beirne, but his matriculation at the late Royal University of Ireland in 1907, and his graduation from University College, Dublin, were both under the name of Bernard Byrne.

APPENDIX

The "Donn" appears in his name for the first time, apparently, soon after his arrival in America. His marriage certificate, dated December 2, 1911, gives the name as Bernard Donn Byrne. According to Mrs. Byrne, the "Donn" was added "to save one from the million other Byrnes in the telephone book." She goes on to add that the word "donn" means "brown" in Gaelic, and that "there is some theory about the Wicklow Byrnes being red and the northern ones brown or dark haired."

"Oswald" appears for the first time in print, so far as is known, in 1912 (biographical notice in Kennerley's *The lyric year*). Why this name was added to the others remains a matter of conjecture. A close friend of Byrne's during the early New York days owned a pet macaw which he called Oswald. Byrne was always intrigued by this bird, and his fancy may have been so taken by it that he adopted the name for himself. In any event, no more plausible explanation has been offered.

In supplying information about himself for *Who's who*, the author gave his name as Brian Oswald Donn Byrne. His vivid imagination and love for the extravagant inspired the claim he made to friends that his true and rightful name was Brian Oswald Pierre Marie D'Arcy Donn-Byrne, O'Byrne. This latter is attested by a close friend of his in the 1912–1915 period, in a personal communication to the writer.

After he became established as a writer, he usually signed his name "Donn Byrne," although in 1913 and 1914 there were occasional lapses into the earlier custom, and the name appeared as Brian (or Bryan) Donn Byrne.

There are occasional references to Byrne which include "Patrick" in his name (as *National cyclopedia of American biography*), or "Percy" (the full name Brian Oswald Percy Donn Byrne was known in Hollywood), and Mr. Greenberg's thesis mentions that at one time he was known as Donald Donn Byrne. An ALS in the writer's possession is signed "Donn Byrne of Oriel."

During the Coolmain period, his personal cards were engraved "Mr. Brian Donn-Byrne"; his gravestone is inscribed DONN BYRNE.

Note 4. Chronology

1889	Nov. 20.	Born, at 337 W. 20th Street, New York City.
	Dec. 1.	Baptized, Church of the Guardian Angels, New York.
1890		Taken to Ireland "at age of three months."
1890–1906		Boyhood spent at Camlough, near Newry, Co. Armagh.
1907	Summer	Matriculated at Royal University of Ireland.
1908	Summer	Passed First University Examination.
1909	Summer	Passed Second University Examination in Arts.
1910	Autumn	Passed B. A. Examination of National University of Ireland.
	Oct. 29.	Admitted to degree of B. A. at University College, Dublin.
		Visited Continent (Paris, Leipzig, etc.).

DONN BYRNE BIBLIOGRAPHY

1911		Came to America and took up residence in Brooklyn. Lived first at 183 Schermerhorn Street, later at 183 Columbia Heights.
	April	Dorothea May Cadogan arrives in New York City.
	August 12.	Starts work with *New Standard dictionary*.
	Dec. 2.	Married, at St. Charles Borromeo Church.
1912	February	"The Piper" in *Harper's*.
		Leaves *New Standard dictionary*; later, works for *Century dictionary*.
		Lectures for Brooklyn Board of Education.
		Secretary of Gaelic Literature Association of America.
		First child, Hedda, born.
1913		Writing for *The Irish American* and for *The Philippine bulletin*.
		Second child, St. John, born.
1914	February	First story, "Battle," in *Smart set*.
		Work on *New York Sun*, *New York Globe*, and *Brooklyn Eagle*.
		Writing for *Snappy stories*, etc.
1915		First book, *Stories without women*.
		Still living at 183 Columbia Heights.
1916	May	Bermuda trip with Mr. J. R. K. Taylor.
		Moves to 15 Clark Street, Brooklyn.
1917	Fall	Moves to Port Jefferson.
1918		Variously at Larchmont, Oak Bluffs (Martha's Vineyard), and New York.
	Nov. 11	Spends Armistice Day with Mr. Richardson Wright.
	December	Reunion with Mr. Taylor in New York.
		Contract with Hearst Publications for one short story per month for 1919.
1919	Spring	Moves to Riverside, Conn.
		Florida trip in January or February (?).
	Oct.	Twins, Jane Olive and Brian Oge, born at Riverside.
	Dec.	SB published.

APPENDIX

1920	Sept.	*FM* published.
		Short stories, motion picture scenarios, etc.
1921		*MMP* written, "in three months"; published in November.
		Work on *WB*, finished Dec. 29th.
1922	April	Leaves U. S. for England (London, Cornwall, Devon, etc.).
	June	Leaves England for Ireland.
	July	At Greythorn, near Kingstown.
	July – Dec.	Travels about Europe, leaving family at Greythorn.
1923	Feb. 1	Moves from Greythorn to Montrose House, Donnybrook.
		Later in year, at Walmer, near Deal.
1924	May	At Newquay, Cornwall; later, visits the continent (Monte Carlo, etc.).
1925	Spring	Visits Holy Land.
	June 9	Arrives in New York for brief visit.
	June 20	Leaves New York for Warren Farm House, Guildford, Surrey.
	August	At Dartmouth, Devon.
1926		Variously at Dartmouth, Brittany, Warren Farm House, Villa Gothique (Cannes), Villa Caplane (St. Cloud, Paris), etc.
1927	Jan.	At Villa Caplane.
	Feb.	South of France, thence to Ireland and Coolmain. Late in year, at Barwell Court, Chessington, Surrey.
1928	April	Leaves Barwell Court for a holiday in France.
	May	Returns to Barwell Court.
	June 15	Arrives at Coolmain.
	June 18	Death, Courtmacsherry Bay.

Milton Keynes UK
Ingram Content Group UK Ltd.
UKHW040040180324
439604UK00006B/887